WORKFARE
vs.
WELFARE

Beverly J. Fanning

IDEAS IN CONFLICT SERIES

502 Second Street
Hudson, Wisconsin 54016
Phone (715) 386-7113

Library of Congress Cataloging-in-Publication Data

Fanning, Beverly J., 1964-
   Workfare vs. welfare.

   (Ideas in conflict)
   Bibliography: p.
   1. Public welfare—United States. 2. Welfare recipients—Employment—United States. I. Title. II. Title: Workfare versus welfare. III. Series.
HV95.F34 1989   362.5′8′0973   88-43117
ISBN 0-86596-072-0

Illustration & photo credits

Chuck Asay 95, Bulbul 57, Carol★Simpson 25, 100, 116, 129, General Accounting Office 12, *The Guardian* 49, Gary Huck 19, Steve Kelley 64, Stuart Leeds 91, Lolinkert 32, Geoffrey Moss 104, 122, *People's Daily World* 73, William Sanders 42, 110, David Seavey 86, U.S. Department of Health and Human Services & the Michigan Department of Social Services 78, Richard Wright 138.

publications inc.

© 1989 by Gary E. McCuen Publications, Inc.
502 Second Street • Hudson, Wisconsin 54016
   (715) 386-7113
International Standard Book Number 0-86596-072-0
Printed in the United States of America

CONTENTS

Ideas in Conflict   6

CHAPTER 1 WORK AND WELFARE: AN OVERVIEW

1. WORK PROGRAMS FOR WELFARE RECIPIENTS:
   AN INTRODUCTION   9
   United States General Accounting Office

CHAPTER 2 WORKING FOR WELFARE: PHILOSOPHICAL ARGUMENTS

2. WELFARE PROGRAMS: SUCCESS OR FAILURE?   22
   John E. Schwarz vs. M. Stanton Evans

3. WELFARE: PROMOTING POVERTY
   OR PROGRESS?   29
   *Richard D. Coe and Greg J. Duncan
   vs. Charles Murray*

4. WORKFARE: IT ISN'T FAIR AND
   IT DOESN'T WORK   39
   Laurie Udesky

5. WORKFARE: A PROGRAM THAT WORKS   46
   Christine Adamec

6. WORKFARE RESTRICTS ACCESS TO
   WELFARE BENEFITS   54
   *Fred Block, Richard A. Cloward, Barbara Ehrenreich,
   and Frances Fox Piven*

7. WORKFARE WILL TRANSFORM
   PASSIVE RECIPIENTS   61
   Lawrence M. Mead

Case Study on Work Programs: Massachusetts' Employment and Training (ET) Choices Program

Overview: Work Programs on the State Level   69

     8. THE MASSACHUSETTS MIRACLE   70
        Michael Dukakis

     9. THE STUNNING FAILURE OF "ET"   75
        Warren T. Brookes

CHAPTER 3 WELFARE REFORM: IDEAS IN CONFLICT

     10. WELFARE REFORM IS A GOOD INVESTMENT   83
        John Ashcroft

     11. WELFARE REFORM WILL BE TOO COSTLY   88
        Peter B. Gemma Jr.

     12. WELFARE NEEDS TO BE REPLACED,
        NOT REFORMED   92
        Ronnie Blakeney

     13. WORKFARE PARTICIPATION SHOULD BE
        MANDATORY   97
        Dorothy Kearns

     14. WORKFARE PARTICIPATION SHOULD BE
        VOLUNTARY   101
        Patrick Conover

     15. WE NEED A NATIONAL WELFARE POLICY   107
        John Larson

     16. LET THE STATES CONDUCT THEIR
        OWN PROGRAMS   113
        William Kohlberg

     17. THE GOVERNMENT IS RESPONSIBLE   119
        Thomas Harvey

     18. THE INDIVIDUAL IS RESPONSIBLE   126
        Douglas Besharov

     19. SOCIETY AND RECIPIENTS SHOULD
        SHARE RESPONSIBILITY   135
        Daniel Patrick Moynihan

Appendix I: Work Program Activities   142

Appendix II: New Welfare Reform Bill   146

Bibliography   147

REASONING SKILL DEVELOPMENT

These activities may be used as individualized study guides for students in libraries and resource centers or as discussion catalysts in small group and classroom discussions.

1. Interpreting Editorial Cartoons   18
2. What Is Editorial Bias?   80
3. Recognizing Author's Point of View   141

IDEAS in CONFLICT ®

This series features ideas in conflict on political, social, and moral issues. It presents counterpoints, debates, opinions, commentary, and analysis for use in libraries and classrooms. Each title in the series uses one or more of the following basic elements:

Introductions *that present an issue overview giving historic background and/or a description of the controversy.*

Counterpoints *and debates carefully chosen from publications, books, and position papers on the political right and left to help librarians and teachers respond to requests that treatment of public issues be fair and balanced.*

Symposiums *and forums that go beyond debates that can polarize and oversimplify. These present commentary from across the political spectrum that reflect how complex issues attract many shades of opinion.*

*A **global** emphasis with foreign perspectives and surveys on various moral questions and political issues that will help readers to place subject matter in a less culture-bound and ethnocentric frame of reference. In an ever-shrinking and interdependent world, understanding and cooperation are essential. Many issues are global in nature and can be effectively dealt with only by common efforts and international understanding.*

Reasoning skill *study guides and discussion activities provide ready-made tools for helping with critical reading and evaluation of content. The guides and activities deal with one or more of the following:*

RECOGNIZING AUTHOR'S POINT OF VIEW

INTERPRETING EDITORIAL CARTOONS

VALUES IN CONFLICT

WHAT IS EDITORIAL BIAS?

WHAT IS SEX BIAS?

WHAT IS POLITICAL BIAS?

WHAT IS ETHNOCENTRIC BIAS?

WHAT IS RACE BIAS?

WHAT IS RELIGIOUS BIAS?

*From across **the political spectrum** varied sources are presented for research projects and classroom discussions. Diverse opinions in the series come from magazines, newspapers, syndicated columnists, books, political speeches, foreign nations, and position papers by corporations and nonprofit institutions.*

About the Editor

Beverly J. Fanning is an editor for GEM Publications, Inc. She has also worked as an editor in state government, law, and the insurance industry. Ms. Fanning graduated from the University of Wisconsin-River Falls with a Bachelor of Arts degree in English and a minor in professional writing.

CHAPTER 1

WORK AND WELFARE:
AN OVERVIEW

1. WORK PROGRAMS FOR WELFARE
   RECIPIENTS: AN INTRODUCTION
   United States General Accounting Office

1

WORK AND WELFARE: AN OVERVIEW

WORK PROGRAMS FOR WELFARE RECIPIENTS: AN INTRODUCTION

United States General Accounting Office

The United States General Accounting Office prepared this report for the chairman of the Subcommittee on Intergovernmental Relations and Human Resources of the House of Representatives Committee on Government Operations. The report responds to the chairman's request for information on employment-related programs for applicants and recipients of Aid to Families with Dependent Children (AFDC) benefits.

Points to Consider:

1. What circumstances prompted the changes in work/welfare programs?
2. Describe the new work program options.
3. Who are the long-term users of AFDC? Why is it difficult for these people to achieve financial independence?
4. How have state work programs become more comprehensive? Provide examples to support your answer.

United States General Accounting Office, *Work and Welfare: Current AFDC Work Programs and Implications for Federal Policy* (Gaithersburg, Maryland: January 1987).

9

Although past proposals for comprehensive welfare reform have met with little success, the idea of changing the welfare system recently has attracted new interest.

Introduction

Over the past five years, state agencies administering the Aid to Families with Dependent Children (AFDC) Program have taken a new look at linking welfare and work. A developing consensus that this link should be strengthened is signaled by the states' interest in work-related programs, renewed as a result of federal legislative changes made in 1981 and 1982. Such programs establish an obligation for participation in return for benefits, an opportunity for recipients to obtain needed skills and education, or both.

Although serving a minority of welfare recipients, some programs—such as California's Greater Avenues for Independence (GAIN) or Massachusetts' Employment and Training (ET) Choices—have received much media attention as approaches to reforming welfare. Although past proposals for comprehensive welfare reform have met with little success, the idea of changing the welfare system recently has attracted new interest. An administration working group has developed a draft report on the welfare system recommending a series of state demonstration initiatives that would include mandatory work programs for welfare recipients. Independent of an overall welfare reform proposal, several specific proposals to replace or alter work program authority have been advanced, including one by the administration and several by members of the Congress.

Although some of the new work programs are well-known and a few studies are available on specific programs, little is known about the programs as a whole. . . .

Most of these programs are not what is commonly known as ''workfare''—work in exchange for welfare benefits—though they are often called by this name. While some programs adopt this approach as their primary activity, others offer it only as one of several activities, which might also include education and training, and still others do not use it at all. This report therefore refers to the programs as a whole as ''work programs,'' not as workfare.

New Work Program Options

The 1981 and 1982 changes in work/welfare programs occurred within the context of concern about increasing AFDC caseloads and expenditures in the 1970s as well as the dramatic increase in labor force participation among women with children during the past 20 years. These changes raised questions about AFDC mothers with children

A POSITIVE DEVELOPMENT

The current work programs are a positive development toward making AFDC something more than an income-maintenance program. While it is inappropriate to generalize from a few programs, evaluations have shown that some programs can help AFDC recipients improve their ability to find jobs and reduce their need for welfare.

United States General Accounting Office, Work and Welfare: Current AFDC Work Programs and Implications for Federal Policy *(Gaithersburg, MD: January 1987),* p. 126

being supported without working, suggesting instead that they should at least be preparing for work. The Work Incentive (WIN) Program, the primary program directed specifically at helping AFDC recipients reduce their need for welfare, had been criticized both for the inefficiency of dual agency administration and for failing to help many welfare recipients leave the rolls.

In 1981, the administration proposed eliminating WIN and requiring states to establish mandatory workfare programs called Community Work Experience Programs (CWEP). The workfare concept was first used in state and local general assistance programs as early as the 1930s, but was prohibited for federally supported programs until 1981, except for special demonstrations. In 1981, however, the Congress allowed states to establish CWEP programs as one of three new work program options authorized in the Omnibus Budget Reconciliation Act (OBRA). . . .

OBRA gave states the option of operating experimental WIN programs administered solely by the AFDC agencies. These "WIN Demonstrations" gave states more flexibility in designing their programs and allocating resources. Most of the services, however, are also available under the regular WIN program. WIN Demonstrations, like the regular WIN program, may offer a range of services including assistance in searching for employment, work experience, and vocational skills training.

By the beginning of fiscal year 1986, 26 states had received demonstration status, accounting for over two-thirds of WIN funding. The WIN Demonstration authority is temporary. The demonstrations may operate for three years from the date of initial approval by the Department of Health and Human Services (HHS), except that those approved before June 30, 1984, can be extended to June 30, 1987. The deadline for all applications for demonstration status was June 30, 1985.

11

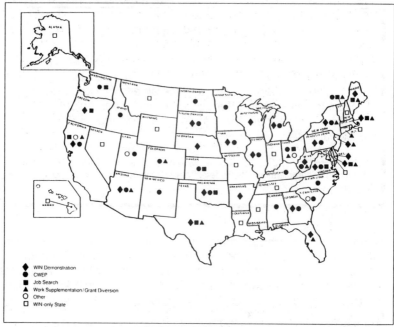

WIN Demonstration
CWEP
Job Search
Work Supplementation/Grant Diversion
Other
WIN-only State

Note: Connecticut, Indiana, and Tennessee started WIN Demonstrations at the beginning of fiscal year 1986, but these programs were not included in our survey.

   A third option authorized by OBRA was work supplementation in which the participant's welfare grant would be used to subsidize a job in a public or private non-profit entity. The Deficit Reduction Act of 1984 (DEFRA) amended this option to permit job development in the private sector. Prior to DEFRA's implementation, similar programs known as "grant diversion" were authorized using waivers permitted by Section 1115 of the Social Security Act. Finally, the Tax Equity and Fiscal Responsibility Act (TEFRA) gave state AFDC agencies a fourth option, employment search, through which they could require applicants and recipients to look for a job either individually or as part of a group. . . .

AFDC Work Program Participants

   In 1985, about 11 million people, or 3.7 million families, received AFDC, the main federal source of cash welfare for families with children. Almost 10 million recipients in 1985 lived in families where there was only one parent—usually a woman. The rest—about 1 million people—lived in families receiving AFDC-UP (AFDC for families where the principal wage earner is unemployed.)[1] Thus, most AFDC work program participants are likely to be women.

   The number of single-parent families on AFDC nearly doubled from 1970 to 1985, growing from 1.8 to 3.4 million. (AFDC-UP families grew at an even faster rate, but accounted for a much smaller number of families.)[2] Increased numbers of single parent families receiving AFDC reflect in part the growth in the number of female-headed families in poverty—78 percent over the same time period. While the poverty rate for persons in female-headed families changed little over this period, it is much higher than that for other families—4 1/2 times that for all other families in 1985.[3]

Recent research using the Panel Survey of Income Dynamics (PSID), a 15-year longitudinal study, estimates that about a quarter of those who ever use AFDC receive it for 10 or more years over time. These long-term users account for almost 60 percent of AFDC recipients at any one time.[4] They use a larger proportion of the total resources and are the most difficult to help. The data indicate that the people most likely to be long-term users are those who

- had never been married when they began receiving AFDC;
- are black;
- dropped out of high school;
- have no recent work experience; or
- entered AFDC when they were very young or their youngest child was less than three years old.[5]

Thus, those who would afford the greatest welfare savings by becoming employed have to overcome the biggest barriers—lack of education and work experience, and child care responsibilities—to achieve financial independence.

Although many women move out of poverty through a change in family structure such as marriage, they have particular problems in becoming self-sufficient through employment. Many women with child-rearing responsibilities do not receive child support or receive less than the full amount awarded them by a court. They enter a job market where women earn less than men. These and other factors such as transportation and child care costs, the economy as a whole, and their lack of education or job skills are problems for women on AFDC who wish to find and keep jobs. . . .

State Work Program Choices

The new options created by OBRA and TEFRA gave the state AFDC agencies much flexibility in designing their work programs, increasing their ability to tailor programs to their own local needs. By 1985, 38 states had selected one or more options, forming 61 different programs. These programs varied in administrative approaches and goals, which ranged from quick reduction in the welfare rolls or enhancement of participants' long-term self-sufficiency to requiring work in exchange for welfare. Creation of these new programs increased the division of work program administration that began with the dual administration of WIN, as AFDC agencies in states with regular WIN programs set up programs of their own.

Overall, the programs depended heavily on federal dollars, although federal/state shares varied across programs. Over 70 percent of the $272 million spent on the AFDC work programs in 1985 came from federal sources. But the most important funding source, WIN, declined by 70 percent from 1981 to 1987. Different program types receive different levels of federal matching funds, which can lead to emphasizing specific program services based on funding availability. . . .

The federal legislative and administrative framework leaves room for the states to set different program goals. Throughout its history, the WIN program has been caught between the goals of (1) immediately reducing welfare expenditures through quick job placements and (2) helping individuals increase their abilities to achieve long-term self-sufficiency by improving their education and skills prior to placement in unsubsidized jobs, which may or may not reduce expenditures more in the long term. The new program legislation has not resolved the tension between these two goals, leaving the choice to state governing officials or individual program administrators.

Either goal is possible within the overall structure of a WIN Demonstration. Job search programs by definition have a goal of quick job placements, while grant diversion or work supplementation programs take a longer term approach by guaranteeing as much as nine months in a subsidized job.

Even a program type such as CWEP with a narrow range of services may have a number of possible goals. CWEP goals may include:

- helping welfare recipients find unsubsidized jobs,
- deterring employable people from going on or staying on welfare,
- providing services of value to local communities in return for their expenditures on welfare, or
- increasing public support for welfare by giving citizens cause to believe that all who can work are doing so. . . .

According to an Urban Institute study, CWEP is most often used to provide limited work experience.[6] We also found states emphasizing workfare's potential in reducing welfare rolls and obtaining work in exchange for welfare. One program that Manpower Demonstration Research Corporation (MDRC) studied even viewed CWEP as a long-term employment program in an environment of high unemployment.[7] . . .

Programs Becoming More Comprehensive

Current work programs build on previous experiences in work program approaches, including job club, supported work, and workfare experiments from the 1970s and their own WIN experiences. The services the programs provide are not new, but the interest and activity in the welfare agency is. We observed states that displayed a process of trial and error, sometimes trying several different approaches on a small scale before implementing a larger program, sometimes starting with a large program and modifying it over time. In general, they have moved toward larger, more comprehensive programs with a wider range of activities including education and training. For example:

- California recently began the Greater Avenues for Independence (GAIN) program, providing job search first for most participants, then services such as work experience and training. This comprehensive program culminated a history of work program experiments, beginning with workfare in the early 1970s and continuing since 1982 with San Diego's job search/work experience program, a grant diversion program, a saturation work program (to achieve high levels of participation or "saturation"), and a WIN Demonstration consisting mostly of job search.

- Initially, Michigan's WIN Demonstration heavily emphasized immediate employment and CWEP. By 1985, the Michigan Opportunity Skills and Training (MOST) program, the product of extensive legislative debate, deemphasized immediate job placement services for AFDC recipients who are not job-ready. Participants lacking education or employment skills were assessed and could be placed immediately in education or training, for which the program had additional funds. The number of people in CWEP had declined almost by half while the number in vocational training almost doubled.

- Massachusetts' original WIN Demonstration, begun in 1982, required welfare recipients to participate in job search before skills training. Participants in this controversial mandatory program often found low-wage, unstable jobs. In 1983, the program was redesigned as the well-known ET Choices, which stressed education and training, and voluntary participation. . . .

Conclusions

A broad look at federal work program options and state choices from among them shows three factors at work in the current work program environment.

1. The variety of services states can provide has allowed states the flexibility to experiment with different approaches over time and develop their programs to accommodate local factors.

2. The complex array of program types—WIN Demonstrations, CWEP, employment search, work supplementation, as well as the regular WIN program—has increased the division of work program policy and administration. Some state AFDC agencies have one comprehensive program encompassing a range of services, while others have several small efforts. In some states all programs are run by the state AFDC agency. Other states have the regular WIN program, in

which the State Employment Security Agency (SESA) provides employment and training services and the AFDC agency arranges support services while also running its own programs. Such an array of program authorizations—created through legislative compromise—is not necessary to provide flexibility. Accommodation of local needs could be provided for in one comprehensive authorization with uniform funding and administration.

3. The future of federal involvement in work programs is uncertain. The WIN Demonstration authority, used by states as a springboard to comprehensive programs such as Massachusetts' ET Choices, California's GAIN, Michigan's MOST, and Illinois' Project Chance, will expire for most states in 1987. Furthermore, federal financial support is declining. WIN funds provided 60 percent of all work program funding in 1985, but have declined by 70 percent in the past six years. Heavy reliance on this source to run the programs could jeopardize their future, if states cannot contribute more resources.

These elements raise questions about future federal and state roles and responsibilities in providing employment-related services to AFDC recipients. The legislation authorizing these programs could be modified to maintain the flexibility accorded to states while decreasing the complexity caused by varying regulations and funding formulas.

---

[1] U.S. House, Committee on Ways and Means, *Background Material and Data on Programs Within the Jurisdiction of the Committee on Ways and Means,* 99th Cong., 2nd sess. (Washington, D.C.: GPO, 1986), p. 391.

[2] *Background Material,* p. 391.

[3] Bureau of the Census, *Money Income and Poverty Status of Families and Persons in the United States: 1985* (Advance Data from the March 1986 Current Population Survey), Current Population Reports, Series P-60, No. 154 (Washington, D.C.: GPO, 1986), pp. 23-24.

[4] David T. Ellwood, *Targeting "Would-Be" Long-Term Recipients of AFDC* (Princeton, NJ: Mathematical Policy Research, Inc., 1986) p. 25.

[5] Ellwood, pp. 41-44. Some of these factors have no impact on welfare receipt in and of themselves, but instead are associated with other factors related to long-term welfare receipt. For example, young mothers are likely to have other characteristics, such as having never been married, associated with long-term welfare receipt. The woman's age has no independent impact on length of time on welfare.

[6] Demetra Smith Nightingale, *Federal Employment and Training Policy: Changes During the Reagan Administration* (Washington, D.C.: The Urban Institute, 1985), p. 80.

7 Judith M. Gueron, *Work Initiatives for Welfare Recipients: Lessons From a Multi-State Experiment* (New York: Manpower Demonstration Research Corporation, 1986), p. 25.

INTERPRETING
EDITORIAL CARTOONS

This activity may be used as an individualized study guide for students in libraries and resource centers or as a discussion catalyst in small group and classroom discussions.

Although cartoons are usually humorous, the main intent of most political cartoonists is not to entertain. Cartoons express serious social comment about important issues. Using graphics and visual arts, the cartoonist expresses opinions and attitudes. By employing an entertaining and often light-hearted visual format, cartoonists may have as much or more impact on national and world issues as editorial and syndicated columnists.

Points to Consider:

1. Examine the cartoon in this activity. (See next page.)

2. How would you describe the message of this cartoon? Try to describe the message in one to three sentences.

3. Do you agree with the message expressed in this cartoon? Why or why not.

Cartoon by Gary Huck. Reprinted with permission of Huck/Konopacki, UE News.

CHAPTER 2

WORKING FOR WELFARE: PHILOSOPHICAL ARGUMENTS

2. WELFARE PROGRAMS:
    SUCCESS OR FAILURE?
    John E. Schwarz vs. M. Stanton Evans

3. WELFARE: PROMOTING
    POVERTY OR PROGRESS?
    *Richard D. Coe and Greg J. Duncan
    vs. Charles Murray*

4. WORKFARE: IT ISN'T FAIR
    AND IT DOESN'T WORK
    Laurie Udesky

5. WORKFARE: A PROGRAM THAT WORKS
    Christine Adamec

6. WORKFARE RESTRICTS ACCESS
    TO WELFARE BENEFITS
    *Fred Block, Richard A. Cloward,
    Barbara Ehrenreich, and Frances Fox Piven*

7. WORKFARE WILL TRANSFORM
    PASSIVE RECIPIENTS
    Lawrence M. Mead

Case Study on Work Programs: Massachusetts' Employment and Training (ET) Choices Program

Overview: Work Programs on the State Level

8. THE MASSACHUSETTS MIRACLE
    Michael Dukakis

9. THE STUNNING FAILURE OF "ET"
    Warren T. Brookes

2   WORKING FOR WELFARE

WELFARE PROGRAMS: SUCCESS OR FAILURE?

John E. Schwarz vs. M. Stanton Evans

John E. Schwarz contends that welfare programs have succeeded. He wrote an article in defense of this position as associate professor of political science at the University of Arizona. He is also author of America's Hidden Success: A Reassessment of Twenty Years of Public Policy *(W. W. Norton & Co., 1983).*

M. Stanton Evans, on the other hand, maintains that welfare programs have failed. He wrote an article defending this position as a contributing editor for Human Events, *a national conservative weekly.*

Points to Consider:

1. What percentage of people lived in poverty during the 1960-80 years? Why were these people poor?
2. In what way did government welfare programs help the poor?
3. According to M. Stanton Evans, how much has social welfare spending increased since 1966?
4. Do you agree with Mr. Evans' conclusion that social welfare spending has hurt the poor? Why or why not?

by John E. Schwarz

A recurring topic of concern in American politics is whether or not to reduce the social programs of government. It is the perception of many people that public assistance programs have grown to be unnecessarily large over the past 20 years, that they have been inefficient, and that their enormous growth has helped promote welfare dependency while also contributing to the dissolution of large numbers of families.

Nary a voice today speaks out loudly in support of the thirtyfold spending increases for the welfare programs in the 1960-80 years. Consequently, it is no surprise that few Americans understand why this very large expansion of the programs was necessary. Yet unless the underlying causes of the spending increases are recognized and kept firmly in mind, intelligent debate cannot proceed on what to do next.

The Need for Social Spending

The need for a significant enlargement of social spending arose partly because two decades ago, in the world's wealthiest economy, 20 percent of the American people still lived in poverty. Even more important, the private economy, no matter how powerfully it grew, was unlikely to brighten this grim picture soon. The reason is that in the years from 1965-80 alone, a net addition of 30 million Americans, a stunning 40 percent increase, entered our work force. This was largely the result of the coming of age of the postwar baby boom and changes in women's attitudes about employment. Even a record-breaking economic performance would not easily meet the huge employment requirements of this avalanche of new job seekers, let alone reach down to help the poor.

Our economic performance was indeed powerful in the 1960-80 years; few realize that our economy's real gross national product (after subtracting for inflation) doubled in these two decades alone; so, too, did our industrial production; and with a 50 percent increase in the provision of new jobs, we set a record unmatched by any other major Western economy in the period.

To what extent did this reach the poor? Even this fine economic performance proved unable to reduce the percentage of Americans living in poverty more than slightly, except for the help of the government's programs, mainly because of the huge influx of labor throughout these years. Census figures tell us that based on the private economy's performance alone, about 20 percent of the American people would still have been impoverished in 1980, a figure barely different from that in 1960 when our economy was about half the size.

On the other hand, until they were cut in 1981-82, the government's programs did reach the poor. Often specifically directed at the impoverished, they managed to reduce poverty significantly. By 1980, if all the programs are included, they pared down the number of impoverished Americans to about 7 percent, marking a reduction of the 1960 figure by almost two-thirds.

Are There Any Side Effects?

However, it is claimed that many offsetting side effects have accompanied this reduction of poverty, effects such as welfare's tendency to promote long-term dependency. But contrary to the common view, only a small minority of families stay on welfare indefinitely. Two-thirds of the families remain on the rolls for fewer than three years, with many reentering welfare only intermittently, generally when economic slowdowns or recessions reappear.

Also, welfare families, with an average of just over two children, do not typically become loaded down with newborns in order to supplement welfare payments. As for the common view that children from welfare families often continue to be welfare dependent into adulthood, the results of the Michigan Survey Research Center analysis of thousands of American families—the foremost study of families in the past two decades—show no evidence that children from welfare families

Q: Why do so many WELFARE recipients drink up their checks?

A: Because they're _still_ on the BOTTLE.

Carol ★ Simpson ©1987

are any more likely to become welfare recipients as adults than are non-welfare children from similar economic circumstances.

Nor have the programs been a central factor behind the breaking up of families. The incidence of family dissolution grew rapidly over the past generation in every income category, not only among families in the income ranks receiving public assistance. Indeed, no alternative to the government's programs has been found to be significantly more successful in holding impoverished families together. This is despite the experiments with many different kinds of direct assistance and guaranteed income substitutes over the past two decades. In many instances, the experiments showed that families might have dissolved with greater rapidity under the alternative programs.

Fooling Ourselves

We fool ourselves if we think that the substantial enlargement of the government's public-assistance programs was somehow unnecessary, or that private economic growth could have sufficed. For the impoverished, this point is brought home with a vengeance today. Virtually every major city in the nation reports that the number of homeless Americans is currently at a peak—the total is thought to approach two million—

notwithstanding the fact that the economic recovery is now a full year running. The lines at soup kitchens have never been longer, either. Because the enlargement of the programs was a necessary response to an unavoidable oversupply of labor—a condition that still exists— further cuts in real spending in the programs can produce only one result: Still more Americans will become impoverished.

by M. Stanton Evans

Among the many abnormalities of the liberal welfare state is the fact that hundreds of billions of dollars in "social welfare" outlays seem to have had no effect, statistically speaking, in getting rid of poverty.

Increased Welfare Spending Has Not Reduced Poverty

The growth of national spending for "social welfare" or "human resource" programs since the era of Lyndon Johnson has been truly astronomical.

In 1966, the national budget for Social Security, Aid to Families with Dependent Children (AFDC), Medicare, and similar functions came to a now paltry-looking $41.8 billion. Last year, the outlay figure for such programs was a staggering $416 billion—almost exactly a ten-fold increase.

You might suppose that such a massive surge in social welfare outlays would have dramatically reduced the number of poor people in our midst. As noted in this space last year ("Losing the War on Poverty," *Human Events,* Aug. 27, 1983), however, the official poverty data tell us otherwise.

In 1966, there were 28.5 million poor people in America, officially defined, amounting to 14.7 percent of the population. In 1982, according to the Bureau of the Census, there were 34.4 million poor people, amounting to 15 percent of the population.

In other words, during a span of 17 years, we increased the national budget for human resource programs 1,000 percent—dishing out some $3.2 trillion along the way—in a supposed effort to eradicate poverty.

Instead, we wound up with even more poor people than we had when we got started, both as an absolute number and as a fraction of the population. Not, all in all, a very impressive record.

Examining the Welfare Program

Contrary to suggestions that aggregate spending for such programs has been cut back under President Reagan (and that this is the reason for the increase in the poverty figures), outlays for these programs have continued moving upward in the Reagan era, rising from $300 billion in 1980 to $345 billion in 1981, $373 billion in 1982, and $416 billion in 1983. Indeed, the rate of increase for such programs (most of which are automatic outlays for "entitlements") has been greater in the past three years than it was under Jimmy Carter.

Get beneath the statistical surface and some of the reasons for this puzzle become apparent. One is that the official poverty figures don't take into account such "in-kind" services as food stamps, Medicaid, and public housing. Figuring in the value of such services, rather than simply counting money income, would obviously raise a lot of people

27

above the poverty line. Another is that substantial "human resource" benefits go to people who aren't impoverished—such as middle-class recipients of Social Security and employees of the federal government.

Despite these facts—in part because of them—continued high and rising poverty rates are a grim reproach to liberal planners. If people started focusing on such data, they might conclude the welfare gurus don't know what they're doing with all those billions, or that the poor people who are supposed to be the beneficiaries are being short-changed by the spenders. Either way, the liberal program comes out looking none too good.

Social Welfare Spending Has Hurt the Poor

In apparent realization of this fact, the Washington *Post* has set out to explain the data—and rehabilitate the program. In an analytical piece by reporter Spencer Rich, the *Post* contends the poverty figures are actually better than they used to be, and this shows the liberal welfare state is working. The nature of the exercise may be seen from this statistical summary:

"The official poverty rate stood at 22.4 percent in 1959. . . .The percentage of Americans living below the official poverty level dropped during the 1960s. In 1965 it had fallen to 17.3 percent. It hovered between 11 and 12 percent in the 1970s and only began rising again in 1980, when a severe recession began. It reached 15 percent in 1982, but was still considerably lower than in 1959."

In fact, this statistical record proves the opposite of what the *Post* is trying to tell us. Note that the bench-mark used to measure progress is 1959—when 39 million Americans, on the official figures, were defined as poor. But the war on poverty legislation wasn't enacted until 1965, and didn't begin to take effect until 1966. Why date the comparison to '59?

The answer is that nearly all the officially measured poverty reduction took place in the period '59-'66, when the number of poor people fell from 39 to 28.5 million (and from 22.4 to 14.7 percent of the population). Everything that has happened since, statistically speaking, is at best a wash. It is only by including the period previous to '66 that any over-all poverty reduction can be shown at all, thereby using the economic record prior to the Great Society to make the war on poverty look good.

The more logical conclusion would of course be the reverse: If poverty fell so sharply before the Great Society, and not at all since then, the obvious inference is that all the social welfare spending has hurt instead of helped.

28

3   WORKING FOR WELFARE

WELFARE: PROMOTING POVERTY OR PROGRESS?

Richard D. Coe and Greg J. Duncan
vs. Charles Murray

Richard Coe is an associate professor of economics at the New College of the University of South Florida. Greg Duncan is a senior study director in the Survey Research Center of the University of Michigan.

Charles Murray is a senior research fellow at the Manhattan Institute.

The Wall Street Journal *invited Mr. Coe and Mr. Duncan to review the findings of Mr. Murray's book* Losing Ground *and invited Mr. Murray to do the same for Mr. Coe and Mr. Duncan's* Years of Poverty, Years of Plenty.

Points to Consider:

1. On what points do Mr. Coe and Mr. Duncan disagree with Mr. Murray?
2. Describe Mr. Coe and Mr. Duncan's position with regard to welfare programs.
3. Summarize Mr. Murray's review of *Years of Poverty, Years of Plenty.*
4. Do you agree with Mr. Coe and Mr. Duncan or with Mr. Murray's interpretation of welfare? Explain your answer.

by Richard D. Coe and Greg J. Duncan

In his book *Losing Ground* (Basic, 1984), Charles Murray carries the neoconservative critique of Great Society social policies to its logical extreme. He argues that the programs launched in the 1960s have not only failed to help the disadvantaged, but have actually created dependency by discouraging work, breaking up families, diluting the quality of education, and promoting out-of-wedlock births. Mr. Murray thinks the U.S. would be better off eliminating all federal welfare programs. "Cut the knot," he urges, asserting that "the lives of large numbers of poor people would be radically changed for the better."

This is strong stuff and calls for convincing evidence to warrant the attention it has received. However, his argument rests primarily on 30 years of annual Census Bureau statistics on poverty, family instability, crime, and employment. Mr. Murray himself notes that such information, obtained from annual cross-sectional surveys, is not well-suited for disentangling causation or even describing the longer-term position of particular population groups. Successive annual counts may show unchanging numbers of welfare recipients or numbers of poor people but cannot reveal whether those numbers are made up of an unchanging group. "What we would really like," he writes, "is a longitudinal sample of the disadvantaged."

In fact, there is such a longitudinal study, and it provides a much clearer view of some of the issues Mr. Murray wishes to address. For the past 18 years, the University of Michigan's Panel Study of Income Dynamics (PSID) has been tracking the economic fortunes of a large representative sample of U.S. families—both the disadvantaged and the advantaged. The PSID does not reach back into the 1950s, as the Census Bureau's data can, nor does it cover all the issues addressed (crime, school quality) or ignored (nutrition, infant mortality) by Mr. Murray, but it does provide a wealth of information on patterns of work, on welfare use, and on family composition changes ever since the Great Society programs were begun. In 10 volumes of detailed analysis, in articles by numerous independent researchers and in the summary book *Years of Poverty, Years of Plenty,* the PSID reveals a picture of economic mobility and of generally benign welfare programs that differs dramatically from *Losing Ground.*

Not a Long-Term Experience

Mr. Murray's attack on the core social programs—Aid to Families with Dependent Children and food stamps—is based on the premise that they foster dependency by discouraging work and marriage and reduce the stigma formerly attached to a life on the dole. He concludes, with regret, that these programs cannot be regarded as insurance against temporary misfortune, nor are they an acceptable means of providing a minimally adequate diet or home environment for needy children.

The facts, as shown by PSID data, are remarkably inconsistent with his assumptions.

Fact: Welfare use is not typically a long-term experience. The typical spell of welfare receipt is fairly short—half extend for periods of no more than two years and only one in six lasts for more than eight years. While 50 million Americans lived in families that received some welfare income during the 1970s only five million could be characterized as persistently dependent on it.

Fact: Most welfare recipients mix work and welfare during the years in which welfare is received. Fewer than half of the people who received welfare, whether for a single year or over many years, relied on it as the source of more than half of their total family income over a given period.

Fact: Welfare dependency is not typically transmitted from one generation to the next. The PSID study of the women who grew up in families that depended heavily upon welfare in the late 1960s and early 1970s found that the vast majority—four-fifths—were not themselves heavily dependent upon welfare once they left home and

"I don't think of myself as being on welfare. I think of myself as being federally funded."

established independent households. For black women, there was no significant link between their welfare status and that of their parents.

Fact: Mr. Murray's assertions notwithstanding, there is no conclusive evidence of strong links between the generosity of existing welfare programs and the incidence of births, divorces, marriages, or remarriages. The most comprehensive study of this issue, by Harvard researchers David Ellwood and Mary Jo Bane, completed after *Losing Ground* was written, concluded that "welfare simply does not appear to be the underlying cause of the dramatic changes in family structure of the past few decades."

In short, typical welfare spells are brief, interspersed with work, do not break up families, and are not passed on from parent to child.

The temporary nature of most welfare spells is part of the much larger picture of economic mobility painted by the PSID data. Ours is clearly a dynamic society in which individual and family economic fortunes undergo substantial change. It can correctly be inferred from these longitudinal data that the longer-term distribution of income and, quite likely, economic opportunity are indeed more equal than single-year figures would indicate. This evidence is fundamentally inconsistent with

Mr. Murray's view that the welfare system invariably produces persistent poverty and dependency.

A Significant Number

A look behind the general mobility shows that these changes are frequently for the better, but some are for the worse and many—favorable and unfavorable—appear to result from events largely beyond the control of the individual. Misfortunes are not limited to the lower end of the income scale; their damaging effects can touch all economic levels. Anyone familiar with the economic circumstances of divorced women and their children, who are nearly three times as likely to fall into poverty as divorced men, or with the consequences of a sudden disability or layoff can corroborate this fact. Given time, however, such setbacks are usually overcome as individuals seize some new opportunity provided by a dynamic society to rebuild their lives. In the meantime, the welfare system provides for the majority of recipients precisely what most Americans, including Charles Murray, believe it should: a temporary safety net to ease the burden of hard times.

The darker side of this picture of mobility is the plight of the individuals left behind in its wake. Even with welfare payments added to family income, more than one-tenth of all children (and nearly half of black children) spent a substantial portion of their childhood in poverty. And while they constituted a small fraction of all those who came into contact with welfare, the number of people spending most of the 1970s in welfare-dependent families was far from insignificant—totaling some five million. Since these long-term recipients tend to accumulate on the rolls, they account for a disproportionate share of total program expenditures.

Why do the parents in these persistently dependent families fail to work their way off welfare? Perhaps, as Charles Murray suggests, the unintended incentives of the welfare system played a role. For many, however, even year-round employment in the jobs typically available to them would fail to lift their families out of poverty. Although we are far from understanding the relative importance of discrimination, unemployment, low skills, child-care availability, and welfare disincentives in this process, there is encouraging experimental evidence from the Manpower Development Research Corporation to indicate that job skills programs offer hope for moving long-term welfare recipients into the labor force.

Where does all this leave the welfare debate? Charles Murray sees welfare as a sinister, debilitating force, creating more poverty than it alleviates. But he and other neoconservative writers have simply failed to digest the emerging facts about the dynamic nature of welfare use. We see the system as an indispensable safety net in a dynamic society, serving largely as insurance against temporary misfortune and providing some small measure of equal opportunity in the home environments of children who, after all, constitute the majority of recipients. Viewed in this light, Mr. Murray's proposal that we eliminate welfare for the good of the poor is a cruel joke at best. Despite the welfare system's flaws, its misdirected initiatives and its potentially perverse incentives, it has in fact provided economic assistance to millions of needy Americans without trapping them into dependency.

by Charles Murray

I was fascinated by the data in *Years of Poverty, Years of Plenty* (University of Michigan, 1984). But the inferences I draw from them are at complete odds with the picture painted by the authors.

Contradictory results do not mean that anyone is trying to lie with statistics. They do not mean that "statistics can be made to say anything." But they do mean that "findings" have to be distinguished from "interpretations." Here are some of the ways in which Richard D. Coe, Greg J. Duncan, and their colleagues (the book summarizes several separate studies) and I can agree on the findings and reach quite different interpretations.

Different Interpretations

Sometimes the difference is as simple, and as unresolvable, as a choice among perspectives. A classic example involves one of the most furiously debated topics about welfare: whether Aid to Families with Dependent Children (AFDC) leads to long-term dependency. The data base that Mr. Duncan et al. use reveals that 48 percent of all women who received AFDC during the study were off the rolls within two years. That is a finding. It has also been used as the basis for claiming that welfare dependency is not a major problem. Now, consider exactly the same data, used to calculate another statistic. Of all women who were on AFDC at one time, 50 percent were in the midst of a spell on it that would last for eight or more years. For a typical year during the study, that translated into roughly 1.6 million families and more than five million people. Which view of the situation do you consider important? Greg Duncan examines such data and sees a situation in which AFDC is providing needed help to people in temporary difficulty. I see an underclass, and worry that the benefits of the short-term help are outweighed by the harm of the long-term dependence. The findings are the same. The interpretations are almost mirror images.

A second source of contradictory results is the straw-man problem, something that has been a constant source of frustration in the debate over *Losing Ground*. Everybody knows what conservatives are supposed to think about welfare—they think the system is loaded with cheats who live contentedly off the dole, and that women have babies so they can get a bigger check. *Losing Ground* is against welfare, therefore it must make the same arguments. The data that Mr. Duncan uses refute such stereotypes, and they by extension are said to refute my book. But they don't, because those arguments are not ones that I actually made.

Losing Ground contends that the reforms of the 1960s—not just reforms in welfare, but reforms that transformed the ways in which "the poor" were treated by government policy—had the combined effect of encouraging low-income youths to put together a varying package of some work, some income from the underground economy, and some welfare. They were not always "poor" as defined by the government's poverty line, but they had become de-coupled from the mechanism whereby poor people in this country historically have worked their way out of poverty. "The problem with this new form of unemployment," I wrote, "was not that young black males—or young poor males—stopped working altogether, but that they moved in and out of the labor force at precisely that point in their lives when it was most important that they acquire skills, work habits, and a work record." Similarly, poor young women were reaching their mid-20s with children but no husband (because they either had never married or had been abandoned), and were consigned to the margins of U.S. society. If I am right, then the results to be predicted correspond very closely to what was actually found by the data that Messrs. Coe and Duncan describe.

A Source of Contradiction

Specifically, I would predict that low-income people who are caught in the trap that *Losing Ground* describes will hover near the poverty line, and not escape into the secure working class. The findings of the data in *Years of Poverty, Years of Plenty* track extraordinarily well with this expectation. Messrs. Coe and Duncan interpret these findings as evidence that people are victims of circumstance, and ask us to consider how much worse things would be if we did not have the income-transfer programs to cushion their bad luck. I have no problem with this interpretation as it applies to the elderly and the disabled. But when it comes to healthy working-age people, I ask whether we are witnessing protection against "bad luck" or a system for *producing* it.

Definitions are another source of contradiction in the argument about both dependency and poverty. The conclusion of *Years of Poverty, Years of Plenty* is that "only two percent of the population could be classified as persistently dependent upon welfare income"—a very small number. When one considers how many of those are elderly or disabled, it seems that there must be hardly any welfare dependency at all among the healthy working-age. But a few paragraphs back I pointed out that about five million people were in families in the midst of at least an eight-year spell on AFDC. Aren't all of them dependent?

It all depends on how one defines "persistently dependent." To me, anyone who gets any welfare at all and would be unable to provide for his family without it is dependent on welfare at that moment. For Messrs. Coe and Duncan, a family is not dependent on welfare unless more than 50 percent of its income is from welfare. To me, anyone (again, healthy and working-age) who gets used to the idea that welfare assistance is an acceptable supplement to earned income is "persistently dependent." For them, the only people who are persistently dependent on welfare income are those who received more than half of their income from welfare during at least eight out of the 10 years of the study. And if you think that definition makes it extremely difficult to be defined as "persistently dependent," consider that in computing "half the income," the book *Years of Poverty, Years of Plenty* ignores Medicaid, housing assistance, child nutrition and unemployment payments— meaning for practical purposes that for Mr. Duncan and his colleagues there can be no such thing as a young, healthy, two-parent family that is welfare-dependent. Even for AFDC mothers, the exclusions discount so much of the welfare package that a long-term AFDC mother who periodically holds a job is likely to be counted as "not dependent on welfare."

An Indiscriminate Mix

In the case of economic mobility, perhaps the most widely publicized topic of *Years of Poverty, Years of Plenty*, the problem is not a misleading definition, but the lack of one. Mr. Duncan and his colleagues measured family income in 1971 and again in 1978, and found a high degree of economic mobility in the U.S., both within a single generation and from parents to children. This is, we assume, good news. "Economic mobility" immediately brings to mind youngsters of poor parents moving into the working class, or people moving from the working class to the middle class, all of which is what the American way is supposed to be about.

But the data offered indiscriminately mix several kinds of mobility. One has to do with a normal earnings profile. Almost everyone is at the bottom of the income distribution at some early moment after setting out on one's own. For blue-collar workers who stay in the work force, the entry-level wage is likely to be extremely low, likely to rise rapidly during the early work years, and then tend to level off. For professionals, graduate school is likely to be a time when one is counted as a separate household (thus qualifying for the book's sample) but has very little income—an income that abruptly jumps after graduation. At any given slice of time, these populations of job entrants and the "about-to-be-affluent poor" comprise some millions of people. A second kind of mobility has to do with marriage. Several million of those who were single in 1971 had formed two-income families by 1978 (70 percent of all married-couple families under the age of 35 were two-income in 1978). For them, it was almost impossible to avoid a dramatic jump up the income-distribution scale.

The limited point here is that the real income of many millions of people rose substantially from 1971 to 1978 for reasons that had nothing to do with Horatio Alger. In light of that, how do we interpret the finding in *Years of Poverty, Years of Plenty* that of the bottom quintile (20 percent) of the family income distribution in 1971, 4.5 percent had moved up at least two quintiles by 1978? The interpretation that Greg Duncan and his colleagues reach is that "[t]hese figures suggest a substantial and perhaps surprising degree of income mobility at the bottom end of the income distribution." I read the same numbers. I look up the national household income distribution in 1971 and 1978 and find that I could go from the bottom quintile to the third quintile if my household income increased roughly $6,000 to $12,000 (in constant 1978 dollars) in the seven intervening years. I make some ballpark estimates of the subpopulations that could be expected to do so as a matter of course. My question is: How could the proportion that moved up be so low? And I am left with another question: Once we subtract the subpopulations moving up because of normal life-cycle trends, how much room is left for the kind of economic mobility we want to see? Unfortunately, their own analysis of the dynamics of income movement within the low-income groups suggests that the answer is very little.

If I were a reader of this and the article by Messrs. Coe and Duncan, I think my reaction by this time would be: Why don't you folks get together and thrash it out? Instead of endlessly giving us conflicting versions of the same data, why not reach some sort of consensus? To this my reaction, and I suspect theirs as well, is: Yes, it is about time we do just that. When we finally get a grip on who the "poor" really are, some major policy disputes will begin to resolve themselves.

WORKING FOR WELFARE

WORKFARE: IT ISN'T FAIR AND IT DOESN'T WORK

Laurie Udesky

Laurie Udesky wrote the following reading in her capacity as a reporter for Pacifica and National Public Radio and as an associate of the Center for Investigative Reporting in San Francisco. Her article originally appeared in The Progressive, *a liberal, monthly publication.*

Points to Consider:

1. Why does the California Coalition for Welfare Rights oppose GAIN?
2. What kinds of jobs are GAIN participants trained for? How many participants will actually leave the welfare rolls?
3. Describe the problems associated with the GAIN program.
4. What happens to a recipient who refuses to participate in GAIN?

It's time that lawmakers create a voluntary jobs-training program and jobs to go with it. A voluntary program would also recognize a parent's right to stay home and take care of her children. The states should do more than pour millions of dollars into programs that "train" people for jobs that don't pay enough to support a family.

A "Success" Story

Romelia Carrillo is a California success story. The mother of three children and a six-year welfare recipient, she landed a job as an on-call dietician's aide through the state's workfare program, GAIN—short for Greater Avenues for Independence. It requires all parents whose children are six or older and who receive Aid to Families with Dependent Children to find jobs or work for their welfare checks. As participants prepare to work, it promises, they will receive transportation, subsidized child care, and up to two years of training and education.

In October 1986, Carrillo was chosen "GAIN Employee of the Month." A brightly colored newsletter published by the social services department in Fresno featured her story. Carrillo, the article reports, "takes two buses to ride to work, but is glad to have a job to ride to. Carrillo . . . is very happy to have her job. She has been trained in many aspects of the hospital food service, including setting up trays, delivering them to tables, clean-up, washing the pots and pans, and putting the dishes away. She is looking forward to a long and steady association with the hospital."

But a talk with Carrillo paints a different picture. The young mother confirms her intense desire to work and be independent of welfare. Her hours are irregular, however, and at times her take-home pay dips to $400 a month. Her monthly expenses, she says, include $330 for rent, $137 for car payments, and $65 to $70 for gas and electricity. The most she has made is $700 a month. "But then," she says, the welfare department "cut off my food stamps, and me and my kids had to live on eggs and potatoes."

After three months on the job, Carrillo, like all GAIN participants, had her child-care subsidy cut off. She then had to squeeze an extra $67 a week for child care out of an already-strapped family budget.

"I'm struggling and I know I can't expect welfare to always pay my way," she says. "But it's been very hard."

Most disturbing is the fear that she'll lose the job overnight. "I like my job," she says, "but I've been late for work several times because one of my children is ill. When you're late to work, they count it as a

THE WORK ETHIC

There is a lot of conversation about the fact that workfare would at least give people some activity and teach them the value of work. Perhaps it should be stated very clearly that virtually all Americans value work. Millions report daily to rather monotonous, difficult jobs that hardly pay a living wage and many whose incomes are more than adequate prefer to work.

When jobs are advertised, thousands line up to make applications. Men and women who have not worked in 20 years identify themselves by their professions and vocations and the homeless and hungry offer to do chores to earn spending money. Americans value work. The work ethic does not need to be taught. It is more likely the case that work needs to be provided for many who cannot find employment.

Excerpted from testimony of Betty L. Williams, director of the Department of Social Policy for United Charities of Chicago, before the House Subcommittee on Public Assistance and Unemployment Compensation of the House Committee on Ways and Means, March 13, 1986

sick day, and I've already used up all my sick time. If one of my children is sick again, I'm afraid I'll be fired."

Her voice drops in concern as she talks about her children. "The kids really miss me; I don't see them that much now."

The scarcity of available child care means she must depend on relatives and informal babysitters when she goes to work. Sometimes child-care arrangements fall through at the last minute.

"A couple of times, I've had to leave the kids alone. It's not good, to leave kids alone. One time my six-year-old flooded the bathtub, and water went all over the carpet in the hall and into the downstairs apartment."

GAIN is supposed to find work for thousands, mostly single mothers on the welfare rolls. Billed as a model program, it has caught the eye of lawmakers across the country. Many politicians, including some Presidential candidates, are looking to GAIN and other similar programs as solutions to the welfare problem. But as the case of Romelia Carrillo demonstrates, it is hardly a solution at all.

More Hype Than Substance

When Republican Governor George Deukmejian signed the workfare bill into law in 1985, he claimed it would "give welfare recipients the tools to break out of the endless trap of welfare dependency."

Cartoon by William Sanders. Reprinted with special permission of NAS, Inc.

Assemblyman Art Agnos, one of the liberal Democrats who joined conservatives in pushing GAIN, calls the program "the most advanced,
progressive, state-of-the-art reform of the welfare system in the nation."
The public is being wooed by slick advertisements produced by Louis
and Saul, a Santa Monica firm that will be paid $1.5 million for selling
GAIN over the next three years.

But the program is more hype than substance. Assemblyman Ernie
Konnyu, the Republican who was the main author of the GAIN legislation, says the program will provide welfare recipients with "training and
self-reliance so they can leave welfare and reduce taxpayer costs."
California, however, has invested neither the planning nor the resources
to make good on these promises. In what may be the best-kept secret
of the campaign year, the state's Department of Social Services
estimates that 97 percent of all GAIN graduates will remain on welfare.
And the kinds of jobs the workfare program offers can barely support
one person, much less a family.

"They're training us to become clerks and busboys," says Kevin Asla-
nian of the California Coalition for Welfare Rights. "It's an assembly line,

and you can't live on those wages. That's why we call this program PAIN—which stands for Painful Avenues to Nowhere."

Low Wages

The lack of well-paying jobs for GAIN graduates also worries John Ritter, GAIN manager for the welfare department in Solano County. "It's a real problem because a single parent with two kids needs at least $8 or $10 an hour just to survive," he says. "But the kinds of jobs we have here are service jobs running $5.05 an hour."

A study by Alameda County, cited by the *San Francisco Chronicle,* backs up Ritter. Welfare recipients with one child would need to earn more than $6.44 an hour just to reach the same standard of living they had on welfare, the study points out. Single parents who work have much higher expenses than do those who stay at home; after starting a job, they may lose most or all of their subsidized food, housing, and medical benefits.

A single mother with two children who receives $716 monthly in welfare benefits, for example, would need to earn twice that to cover the added cost of child care, transportation, payroll taxes, and other new expenses. That amounts to a $9.25-an-hour job to reach the same subsistence standard of living she had on welfare—a wage far higher than that earned by most GAIN graduates. California's Department of Social Services reports that the median wage for GAIN employees is $5 an hour. In some counties, it drops as low as $4.

"You can't find a better job until you start with $5 an hour," says GAIN deputy director Carl Williams. "This program has everything conceivable to help people get work, but it's unlikely that unskilled, or modestly skilled, people can get $10 an hour at their first job."

GAIN's low wages reflect a Catch-22 problem with workfare nationwide: A recent federal report on programs in thirty-eight states reveals that most participants were forced to take dismally low-paying jobs, with a median hourly wage of $4.14. Unsurprisingly, fewer than 50 percent of participants were able to get off welfare after finding work.

Workfare Does Not Help People Out of Poverty

This finding is not news to Dion Aroner, an aide to Assemblyman Tom Bates, a long-time critic of workfare programs. Bates opposes GAIN, says Aroner, because it is "not voluntary" and sets aside no money to develop jobs.

"Its creators didn't see it as a way to get families out of poverty," Aroner says. "They saw it as a way to get them off the welfare rolls."

Yet the program is not succeeding in doing even that. With workfare under way in sixteen counties, GAIN has found jobs for only 3,788 of its 27,800 participants. And although the state expects to spend more than $200 million a year on workfare, realistic welfare officials expect few GAIN participants to leave the welfare system. Asked how GAIN's single parents will be able to support a family on $5 an hour, deputy director Williams says, "Your question assumes people will be leaving welfare. We don't expect everyone to leave welfare." He explains that many workers will be eligible for reduced benefits. Pressed further, Williams estimates that only 3 percent of GAIN graduates will be able to make it off the welfare rolls.

Holly Bailey of San Mateo is among this lucky 3 percent. A thirty-five-year-old former welfare mother, Bailey was able to finish her nursing program through GAIN. "When I was getting welfare," she says, "it seemed like you were penalized for trying to go to school and do better in your life. But GAIN has been wonderfully supportive." The program paid for her child care, transportation, and two uniforms, she says. "It really made a difference to have that support."

Bailey now earns $1,800 a month as a registered nurse.

More typical, though, is the case of Linda Carevich, a mother in her thirties who enrolled in GAIN voluntarily in November 1986. With a high-school education and two children, she hoped to get a job as a laborer or some other position that pays well.

"We need to get the kinds of jobs men get and get paid what they get paid," she says. At her GAIN orientation, however, Carevich says she was told to apply for entry-level clerical jobs, bank-teller and child-care aide positions, and other low-paying jobs.

"I thought, 'They've got to be kidding!'" says Carevich. "I don't see how a woman like myself with two kids can get a $5-an-hour job and still pay for child care and medical expenses. It's my children who would suffer. We'd be better off on welfare."

Licensed child-care facilities with openings are scarce or nonexistent in many parts of the state, and that presents another problem for GAIN mothers, even though program administrators downplay it. Williams says he has heard "child-care shortages talked about *ad nauseam,* but I haven't heard of people who have had a problem.". . .

Workfare Has Been Oversold

Faltering start or not, GAIN supporters are quick to defend the program, citing the nonmonetary benefits.

"This program destroys the myth that people on welfare are lazy, shiftless, and don't want to work," asserts Assemblyman Agnos, who is now running for mayor of San Francisco. "The large number of people volunteering for the program has already ended that debate.

"We now have people who are trained, willing, and ready to work," says Agnos. "The question is, can the economy handle them?". . .

As things now stand, many women and men in GAIN must take the job that the welfare department thinks they should, even if it means earning less than their net income from welfare. If they refuse and lose their appeal in a lengthy "conciliation process," they can lose their aid.

Defending sanctions against GAIN parents who miss classes or refuse to take a job without "good cause," Assemblyman Agnos goes so far as to compare welfare mothers to school-aged children. Some women must be forced to participate in GAIN, he says, "just as we do with [children] in public education." A woman who balks "will lose her adult right to spend her [welfare] check as she chooses. The state will handle all her money." If, after three months, the woman is "still recalcitrant"—GAIN literature calls her a "second-time offender"—Agnos says, "she will lose the adult portion of her grant."

Such sanctions are under challenge by the Western Poverty Law Center, which has filed suit charging that a GAIN participant has the right to refuse a job if it means a net loss in income. It is illegal to force parents in GAIN "to take a job where the net income does not meet the basic needs of themselves and their children," concludes the complaint.

The GAIN program has been badly oversold, according to Casey McKeever of the Law Center. "For many people," he says, "GAIN will provide some useful services, such as education and job searches, and give them more self-confidence. But the program is incapable of helping the poor in general. It promotes jobs, but doesn't create them. It doesn't take into account the trend away from union jobs that have provided security to families for generations, and the trend toward service jobs with no security and often no benefits."

McKeever thinks GAIN may create a secondary work force easily exploitable by employers who could reduce wages, "knowing that women and men in GAIN must take the job even if it pays less than their welfare checks."

Whatever the good intentions, GAIN has little to distinguish it from unsuccessful workfare programs in other states. It's time that lawmakers in California and elsewhere create a voluntary jobs-training program and jobs to go with it. A voluntary program would also recognize a parent's right to stay home and take care of her children. The states should do more than pour millions of dollars into programs that "train" people for jobs that don't pay enough to support a family.

If, as Governor Deukmejian says, "workfare is a bridge, and all you have to do is cross it," we ought to make sure the bridge is leading somewhere.

5 WORKING FOR WELFARE

WORKFARE:
A PROGRAM THAT WORKS

Christine Adamec

Christine Adamec wrote the following reading in her capacity as a freelance writer. Her article originally appeared in Conservative Digest.

Points to Consider:

1. What kind of work do workfare participants perform?
2. What percentage of San Diego voters favored denying welfare benefits to able-bodied recipients who refuse to work in return for welfare benefits?
3. Is workfare cost-effective? Explain your answer.
4. Does workfare do anything for the actual workfare participant? Please be specific in your answer.

Christine Adamec, "Workfare Works," *Conservative Digest,* March 1983, pp. 44-45. Reprinted with permission of *Conservative Digest.*

"Workfare could work anywhere if they're willing to make it a human skills program, and try to help the individual become self-sufficient; providing training on how to get a job, and helping people obtain the skills they need to get a job."

Should able-bodied people be required to work for their food stamps? Congress has decided that communities throughout the nation should make this decision for themselves, and operating regulations for establishing workfare programs became effective in November 1982.

Should your community start its own workfare program? How could you know if it would be feasible in your area? Consider the following experiences of people who've actually administered their own workfare programs.

Workfare "Pilot Programs"

Fourteen sites nationwide ran workfare "pilot programs" between 1980 and 1981, and the six sites described in this article represent a cross-section of the U.S., including New Hampshire, California, Virginia, South Carolina, Missouri, and Indiana. Five of the sites continue to operate workfare programs, while the site in Indiana dropped workfare in early 1982.

These sites are diverse, from small town areas such as Tazewell County, Virginia, with an estimated population of 50,000; to highly urban San Diego County, California, which encompasses a population of nearly 2 million. Yet all of the sites shared the same basic regulations governing their program's administration—workfare participants were only assigned to work in jobs at non-profit agencies, and for a specified number of hours per month.

Each "household" (a group of people living together, not necessarily related) receives an amount of food stamps depending on the size of the group. For instance, a group of two people currently receives $139 in stamps. That amount is divided by the minimum wage to determine the monthly work commitment. In that same two person household, one person would have to work 41 hours. Elderly people, disabled people, and mothers with young children are exempt from working.

More People Are Complying

At all sites, some food stamp recipients have refused to work for no good reason. A young man kicked in the city welfare office door in Nashua, New Hampshire when he found out he'd have to work for the stamps he'd previously been receiving free. He was "sanctioned,"

A WORKFARE ELEMENT IS A GOOD IDEA

I think workfare makes sense because of the changed demographics, and the changed role of women in society and the workforce. When the AFDC program was founded women were generally expected to be home with their children, and this is why the system was set up, to enable women to be home with their children. Today when more than half of the mothers of young children work, when many women want to work, many don't but have to, it is an anomaly to have a welfare system which treats a certain segment of women differently from how women are behaving generally in society.

I think in the 1980s, having a workfare element or work component in welfare is healthy for the individual. It is not only good for the budget, it is not only good for society but it is healthy for the individual herself to be earning her own way, to feel that she has the potential for earning her own way. I think if you read various evaluations of welfare programs, that most of the recipients who do participate in work programs are very pleased. The reactions of the recipients to workfare, even straight workfare in a state like West Virginia, are very positive. They think it is fair. They are proud of it, and I think it has real benefits for the recipients as well as for the budget.

Excerpted from testimony of S. Anna Kondratas, Schultz Senior Fellow in Health and Urban Affairs at The Heritage Foundation, before the House Subcommittee on Public Assistance and Unemployment Compensation of the House Committee on Ways and Means, May 22, 1986

meaning his food stamps were cut off for one month because he had no valid reason for *not* working.

The San Diego site cuts nearly 300 people per month off food stamps because they refuse to work, for an estimated annual cost savings to the federal government of over $200,000. Every site has sanctioned people, and new regulations are even stricter—now the whole household will go off for two months if a recipient refuses to work.

Joan Zinser, Project Director of workfare in the San Diego site, says that more people are starting to comply with the program, and 60 percent reported to their worksite in June 1982, as compared to 48 percent in July 1981. She also thinks that compliance will increase, thanks to the new regulations cutting off the entire household for two months, rather than just one person for one month. "I think this is a very good provision," agrees Tazewell County workfare coordinator Lowell Sex-

ton, ''now the recipient will receive motivation to comply from his own family.''

Workfare has also served as an effective screener of frauds. As one administrator put it, "We get suspicious when they can *only* come for their workfare interview between noon and one, or after 5 o'clock." Jean Field—Nashua, New Hampshire's City Welfare Director—describes one of her first workfare cases: a young man and woman who'd been living together and collecting food stamps for over a year, both supposedly unemployed. They came in for their workfare interview on Friday, and then on Monday called Field to report they'd found jobs, and would no longer be needing food stamps, thank you.

Participating in a Variety of Work Activities

What kind of work do participants perform? Do they break rocks or maybe dig holes and then fill them in? At the more than 500 work locations in San Diego, California, participants have done everything from mundane clerical work to setting up dance classes to repairing car radios. As at the other sites throughout the country, work assignments are geared as much as possible to an individual's job skills.

In Tazewell County, Virginia coal country, workfare participants have been used as lab technicians, bulldozer drivers, and rescue squad workers.

In the Greenville, South Carolina site, says workfare program director Marion Graham, "they work in hospitals, deliver meals-on-wheels to elderly shut-ins, act as teacher aides, and work in the library and museum."

In Nashua, New Hampshire, an unemployed Cordon Bleu chef taught cooking to the Girls' Club, and a skilled carpenter repaired the Children's Home so it could pass the fire inspection.

All of the six sites report that the majority of their workfare population is male, but the average age varies from a low of 25 in New Hampshire to a high of 38 years in South Carolina. Average education levels were about constant, ranging from that of the tenth grade education to a high school graduate. Minorities did not appear to be a disproportionate number of participants, although many of these sites are heavily white.

The Need for Community Support

Community support is a critical factor in the success or failure of any workfare program. Most of the six sites report very favorable community support. According to Zinser of San Diego, the voters of San Diego County were asked the following question on their November 4, 1980 general election ballots: "Should the county of San Diego, where legally possible, deny welfare benefits to able-bodied recipients who refuse to perform work in return for welfare benefits?" Eighty-nine percent of the voters answered with a resounding *yes.*

New Hampshire city welfare director Jean Field says she had problems with the state welfare office headquarters. "They found countless reasons why workfare could never work," Field explains. "But the Mayor wanted workfare, the city wanted it, I wanted it, and the U.S. Agriculture Department supported us. We won."

The Tazewell county, Virginia site also experienced some initial difficulties with another agency. According to Harold French, director of the Department of Social Services, "Legal Aid people opposed our program and interfered as much as they could, but our problems with them have subsided."

Chet Dixon—Springfield, Missouri's director of the Department of Human Resources—oversees Greene County's workfare program. (The county has an estimated population of about 185,000, with about 250 people participating in workfare in any given month.) "Sixty-seven percent of those assigned do actually work. This is a very high rate compared to other sites," says Dixon. He thinks Congress should make up its mind whether or not workfare should be an "intervention" program, an option he favors.

"Workfare could work anywhere," he says, "if they're willing to make it a human skills program, and try to help the individual become self-sufficient; providing training on how to get a job, and helping people obtain the skills they need to get a job."

As to bureaucratic red tape, South Carolina's Graham says, "We found the paperwork very manageable." According to Dixon of Missouri, "The paperwork is quite a lot, but we can handle it."

Workfare Is Cost-Effective

Is workfare actually cost-effective? Liberal groups such as "Jobs Watch" in Washington are mounting legal challenges to workfare programs nationwide. They insist not only that workfare is *not* cost-effective, but they contend workfare jobs are primarily composed of make-work jobs or jobs taken away from other workers.

All workfare administrators interviewed disagreed with this assessment. They insist administrative costs are far less than the value returned from workfare programs, both in work performed, and in money saved when people go off food stamps as a direct result of workfare. "Most people would rather work for money," says Field of New Hampshire. . . .

Not only do the workfare administrators think that workfare is cost-effective, they also disagree with liberals' "make-work" accusations. According to Graham of South Carolina, "Our school budget is getting cut by a million and a half dollars, and if workfare people don't do some of the work for the school, then it just won't get done."

Says Indiana's Dorsey, "Workfare doesn't take jobs away from people. It provides a return to the taxpayer, and it's in line with the work ethic of our country." Even though Indiana has dropped workfare, he adds, there's a strong movement afoot to reinstitute the program.

Should Workfare Be Mandatory?

If workfare *is* truly cost-effective, then shouldn't it be mandatory everywhere? Workfare administrators disagree. Said Virginia's French, "I think workfare should be mandatory everywhere because able-bodied people should have an obligation to return something to the taxpayers in exchange for their benefits."

San Diego officials also strongly favor making workfare a mandatory program—in part because of the observable deterrence value of the program, discouraging many who don't want food stamps if they must work for them.

San Diego points to their 14 percent drop in food stamps cases, compared to a mere 2 percent drop in the rest of California, where there were no workfare programs.

Indiana's Dorsey is not so sure workfare could work everywhere. "In some areas, the logistics and costs of workfare could be excessive," he says. "It depends on how the program's implemented."

"In some areas, the cost of transporting workers might not make it cost-effective," adds Graham. Field thinks the program should be voluntary for a different reason: "I wish I could say yes, it should be mandatory, but I'd worry about workfare being institutionalized, and becoming just another square-filler. Workfare works now because we're committed to making it work, we really want it to work. Could it still work if it were mandated? I have serious doubts."

She may have a point. A recent Congressional Research Report on workfare discusses the importance of administrators' attitudes—citing instances when several AFDC programs mandated workfare, but administrators were opposed to the concept. The programs failed. Commenting on two AFDC workfare programs, the report says, "Studies of the California and Massachusetts demonstrations have concluded that their low rates of assignments to workfare projects were not due to program designs but to problems of implementation." In other words, it was shoved down their throats, they didn't like it, and they wanted it to fail—so it did.

According to Dixon, an essential factor to the success of a workfare program is "an honest effort to test the concept."

Workfare Restores Self-Confidence

Does workfare do anything for the actual workfare participant? Administrators noted cases in which food stamp recipients considered themselves unemployable, but found out they could work when they began their workfare job. Self-confidence regained, they went out and found a "real" job.

What about the "dignity" liberals are always telling us we should "give" people? If there's any way to "give" someone dignity and self-respect, workfare is it. "I don't feel guilty anymore about receiving the stamps, because I'm working for them," said one man.

"I don't feel like a charity case anymore," said another.

In addition, the public respects a man or woman who's actually working for his stamps, rather than sitting at home. Notes Dixon, "From observations in Springfield, workfare clients generally appreciate the opportunity to work and even though many initially resisted having to work, their resistance subsided once they began participating."

Even academicians are starting to take a serious look at welfare. A *Wall Street Journal* editorial quoted political professor Lawrence Mead of New York University: "Programs should try to assure recipients the same balance of rights and obligations that non-dependent people face."

If all this sounds reasonable, maybe workfare could work in your community.

6   WORKING FOR WELFARE

WORKFARE RESTRICTS ACCESS TO WELFARE BENEFITS

Fred Block, Richard A. Cloward, Barbara Ehrenreich, and Frances Fox Piven

Fred Block is a professor of sociology at the University of Pennsylvania.

Richard A. Cloward is a professor of social work at Columbia University. He also co-authored, with Frances Fox Piven, Regulating the Poor *and* Poor People's Movements.

Barbara Ehrenreich is the author of several books, including The Hearts of Men *and* Re-making Love.

Frances Fox Piven is a professor of political science at the Graduate University of New York.

Points to Consider:

1. What kind of protection does the welfare state offer?
2. The authors refer to the American welfare system as an uneasy compromise. Why?
3. How will changes in the American economy affect the future employment situation?
4. Why do the authors oppose workfare?

The need for an expanded and reformed welfare state has perhaps never been greater, but the ideological opposition to the welfare state has never been so intense, so well organized, and so powerfully represented.

Over the last decade, the welfare state has become the target of a concerted ideological attack. From the expanding network of conservative think tanks and foundations on up to the president himself, the same themes are reiterated: that social welfare measures are a drag on the economy, an incentive to immorality, and a cruel hoax on the needy themselves. In the process, even the phrase "the welfare state" has been discredited. Conservatives employ it as a term of invective, while liberals, the former advocates of the welfare state, have been hesitant to defend it.

Welfare Provides Protection

What has been momentarily forgotten, in the disarray created by the conservative attack, is that the welfare state is the only defense many people have against the changes and variations of the market economy. Capitalism, from the beginning, has confronted people with the continual threat of economic dislocation: downturns in the business cycle periodically throw millions out of work; shifting patterns of investment plunge some regions (or industries) into depression while others boom; long-term structural changes in the economy—such as the shift away from agriculture and, more recently, from heavy manufacturing—leave millions stranded with obsolete skills and scanty resources. The only sure "logic" of the market is change and disruption; and for many of us, the only protection lies in the programs of the welfare state.

Thus, for example, unemployment insurance and other income maintenance programs alleviate the impact of the business cycle. Medicare and Social Security help the elderly survive in an economy that has little use for them. A host of special programs protect children and single mothers from destitution. Whatever its shortcomings, the American welfare state has blunted the most damaging effects of the market economy; and this alone represents an enormous human achievement.

The conservative assault has also generated confusion about just *whose* achievement it is. To listen to the current, one-sided discussion, one might conclude that social welfare programs had been created *de novo,* some twenty or so years ago, by a handful of "new class" professionals in the universities, foundations, and federal bureaucracies. In fact, the modern welfare state is the product of decades of political effort by ordinary Americans to gain some control over their lives in

WORKFARE: A WEAK SOLUTION TO A BIG PROBLEM

Workfare, also known as Community Work Experience, is a system of forced work. Recipients of public assistance who are considered to be "able-bodied" are required to "work off" their benefits at tasks and sites assigned by the welfare department in public or nonprofit agencies. The number of hours of labor is determined by dividing the welfare benefits by the minimum wage or, less often, by the prevailing wage. . . .

Workfare can appeal to something people believe in, the idea that people should earn their own way whenever possible. But the reality is that workfare does not help build economic independence, and does not offer real work. Instead, it hurts people who are presently working or seeking work as well as people who need public assistance to survive. Workfare ignores the fact that the vast majority of recipients of public assistance want to get off welfare and into real jobs that will enable them to support themselves and their families.

Sequoia, *April-May 1987*

the face of massive economic disruptions. The foundations of the welfare state were laid in the Great Depression of the 1930s, when millions of Americans struggled to win the most basic forms of economic protection: the right to unionize, minimum-wage laws, business regulation, and income support programs such as unemployment insurance. The next period of welfare state expansion was in the 1960s, when black Americans uprooted by the rapid modernization of southern agriculture demanded and won greater protections for the very poor, including increased income benefits, job programs, and health insurance.

The impact of these welfare state programs extends far beyond their immediate beneficiaries. For all of us, in many ways, life has been made a little more humane through the protection of the elderly, the disabled, the young, and the very poor. Working people, in particular, benefit from the existence of a "safety net" that helps shield them from the harsh terms employers often seek to impose in a market economy, especially during periods of economic downturn and uncertainty. Without a safety net, low-paid, unorganized workers would face the choice of passively complying with employer demands or risking joblessness and its traditional consequence—hunger. Even better-paid unionized workers depend on the welfare state to guarantee that periodic mass layoffs will not lead to destitution and homelessness. Thus the welfare state is an achievement not only because it reduces the misery of a

minority in need, but because it eases the chronic insecurity of the majority.

American Welfare System: An Uneasy Compromise

Yet the American welfare state is in many ways a flawed and fragmented creation, especially when compared to the more generous welfare states of the European capitalist societies. The inadequacies of our welfare state reflect a second historical factor in its formation: American social programs were shaped not only by the struggles of poor and working people but by the relatively greater resistance of business in the United States. We have an inadequate, patchwork system of health insurance (Medicaid for the poor, Medicare for the elderly, and so forth) because medical business interests have successfully opposed a comprehensive, universal system of national health insurance. We have grossly inadequate, subpoverty income support programs (especially Aid to Families with Dependent Children) because employers have successfully fought to keep benefits below the minimum-wage level. In general, welfare state programs represent an uneasy compromise between the demands of the economically vulnerable and the resistance of the economically powerful.

The current ideological attack on the welfare state is a continuation of the repeated efforts of the American business elite to limit the gains not only of the most vulnerable, but of the majority of working people. In fact, the contemporary arguments against the welfare state are remarkably similar to those that have been employed decade after decade by business interests and their intellectual representatives. As in the past, they warn that any interference with the "laws" of the market harms the very people who were intended to benefit: limit the prerogatives of employers—through minimum-wage legislation, health and safety standards, or unemployment insurance—and you will slow economic growth, reducing prosperity for everyone. Attempt to help the most needy and you will only succeed in undermining their morality, family life, and self-respect. And so forth. The arguments are ancient and reflect the historic clash of interests that has shaped the welfare state itself.

Economic Circumstances Are Changing

But if the ideological attack on the welfare state echoes the past, the economic circumstances that it grows out of are new and deeply challenging. The American economy is undergoing a structural transformation which may turn out to be as profound in its consequences as the earlier shift from an agricultural to an industrial economy. One element of this transformation is the "globalization" of the economy, as capital becomes increasingly mobile and as foreign competition directly challenges core American industries such as autos and steel. Another element is the new computer technology, which holds both the promise of vastly increased productivity and the threat of massive job loss. For better or for worse, we are headed toward a postindustrial economy in which the kinds of jobs that have traditionally been the mainstay of the American working class will be scarce or nonexistent.

The central political question, then, is who will bear the hardships associated with the transition to a postindustrial economy. Will the new technology and new international division of labor lead to an improved standard of living for the average person—for example, through shortened and more flexible hours of work? Or will the final result be widespread poverty and desperation?

Already, the business community has made its answer plain. It has launched a broad-scale attack on working-class standards of living, including intensified union-busting, demands for concessions in wages and benefits, and the imposition of a greater tax burden on the poor and the middle class relative to the rich. At the same time, business has accelerated the decline of American industry by recklessly diverting capital away from productive investments and into financial speculation. As a result, the class contours of American society have begun to change for the first time in the post-world war era: the affluent control a greater share of wealth and income than ever before; the poor are becoming both poorer and more numerous; and the middle class, faced with stagnating wages and diminishing middle-income employment, is shrinking.

The current attack on the welfare state is of a piece with the overall business offensive against labor. While employers have been pressing for concessions from their workers, business interests have supported an administration that is openly hostile to the welfare state. Thus, precisely at a time when the jobs and industries that once provided economic security to American workers are vanishing or endangered, so too are the social programs that have offered at least some guarantee of subsistence in hard times. Just as we embark on what could be a turbulent transition to a new kind of economy, with the possibility of even more plant closings and unemployment, we have become, as a nation, least prepared to endure the shock of transition without extensive human suffering.

Herein lies the tragedy of our present circumstances. What we need is no less than a new social compact to enable people to cope with a rapidly changing economic environment. What we are likely to get, if conservative business interests prevail, is a return to the untrammeled market as the singular organizing principle governing the lives of poor and working people. The need for an expanded and reformed welfare state has perhaps never been greater, but the ideological opposition to the welfare state has never been so intense, so well organized, and so powerfully represented.

Welfare Reform and Workfare

The strength of the opposition is nowhere better reflected than in current discussions of "welfare reform" that center entirely on workfare— plans to drop individuals from the welfare rolls unless they agree to take available employment or sign up for training programs. There are differences between the various workfare plans with respect to the quality and quantity of the training opportunities offered, the level of coercion in requiring individuals to take particular jobs, and the determination of how quickly a mother must agree to place her small children in child care so that she can participate in work or training. Yet all of the workfare plans reinforce the dominance of the market by pressuring participants to take whatever jobs happen to be available, at whatever wages employers see fit to offer.

The current fixation on workfare as the the the solution of poverty is ironic in view of the fact that a growing number of the poor are working full time at jobs that do not pay enough to keep families above the poverty level. Moreover, forcing hundreds of thousands of welfare recipients into an already overcrowded labor market will only weaken further the economic position of low-wage workers. Supporters of workfare rarely address the fact that the unemployment rate is approximately 7 percent, and has remained at that level even during the expansionary phase of the business cycle. Yet workfare advocates always emphasize that they want to put an end to dependency by allowing the poor to earn a paycheck. No mention is made of the debilitating effects of dependency on the low-wage labor market, though there is nothing ennobling about being forced to please an employer in order to feed one's children. The same can be said of the periodic bouts of involuntary unemployment that are a routine feature of the lives of most low-wage workers.

Yet liberals have been in the forefront of recent calls for workfare. In general, liberals have offered only timid and infrequent rebuttals to conservative attacks on the welfare state. Instead of advancing a strong and principled defense of the welfare state, liberals seem to have fallen into theoretical and moral disarray. Part of the problem lies with the liberal intelligentsia, who were totally unprepared for a re-emergence of conservative opposition to the welfare state. They had, we believe, succumbed to a kind of complacency bred by theory. Most analysts, whatever their other disagreements, had come to take for granted that expanded welfare state programs were an inevitable concomitant of economic growth and urbanization. Consistently, and not unreasonably, a good deal of the work done by left and liberal social welfare analysts was critical of the programs, fastening on their inadequacies and neglecting their achievements. This critical tradition—which certainly had its place in periods of social welfare expansion—left many of the liberal intelligentsia unprepared to respond to the conservative assault with a strong defense of the welfare state.

An Intellectual Vacuum

But this alone cannot account for the failure of former liberal intellectuals to rise to the defense of the welfare state. There has also been an undeniable element of spinelessness in the face of the renewed fashionability of right-wing or "neoconservative" ideology. To be sure, liberal academics reject the simplistic slogans of the right, but just as often they have been willing to jump on the bandwagon, preaching the virtues of "free enterprise" or the merits of workfare as a solution to poverty.

The consequences of this intellectual vacuum have been serious. Many ordinary people, in a variety of circumstances, have organized to protect themselves from the rightward drift of public policy and the business offensive against labor: industrial workers have attempted to resist plant closings and wage concessions; farmers have fought against foreclosures; women's groups have fought to preserve social programs whose beneficiaries are largely women and their dependent children. But all of these efforts have been weakened by the absence of an intellectual framework to give them coherence and legitimacy. Struggles have remained disconnected, and for the most part narrowly defensive, lacking a positive agenda beyond the preservation of the status quo. An ideological framework for resisting the right need not, of course, come from intellectuals alone. But it is difficult for any social group to develop a coherent alternative to the rightward drift when not only the business elite and the government but also the intelligentsia agree that it is futile to oppose the logic of the market.

7 WORKING FOR WELFARE

WORKFARE WILL TRANSFORM PASSIVE RECIPIENTS

Lawrence M. Mead

Lawrence M. Mead wrote the following article in his capacity as associate professor of politics at New York University and as the author of Beyond Entitlement. *His article appeared in* Commentary, *a monthly publication of the American Jewish Committee.*

Points to Consider:

1. Why has AFDC been the main object of welfare reform?
2. How have conservatives influenced welfare reform?
3. What percentage of AFDC cases stay on the welfare rolls more than two years? What percentage remain five years or longer?
4. Summarize the author's opinion of *The Mean Season.*

*One might suppose that radical authors would sup-
port firm measures to transform inert recipients of
welfare into workers who would have more capacity
to press for change. But* **The Mean Season** *opposes
workfare as just another conservative device to restrict
access to aid.*

Welfare reform, one of the hardy perennials of American politics, has
been revived in Washington. Since President Reagan announced his
intention to reform welfare two years ago, proposals have come from
all sides, and bills are now pending in Congress. But the politics of
welfare has altered: where in the past controversy centered on the issue
of expanded benefits, today debate has shifted mostly to "workfare"—
i.e., proposals requiring that adult welfare recipients work or otherwise
better themselves in return for support.

Reforming Welfare

Today, as formerly, the main object of reform is Aid to Families with
Dependent Children (AFDC), the program that supports poor single
mothers and their children, using both federal and state funds. There
are other important federal welfare programs, such as Medicaid and
Food Stamps, which finance health care and food for the poor, yet AFDC
is the focus because dependency on this program seems the most in-
tractable. In fact, what is now known as the "welfare crisis" goes back
to the late 1960s and the early 1970s, when the AFDC rolls more than
doubled, from around five million to over eleven million people, a level
that has since changed little.

In those years, AFDC became entangled with the issues of race and
the inner city. Growing welfarism coincided with other signs of urban
disarray—a rising incidence of female-headed families, illegitimacy,
joblessness, troubled schools, and crime. Just when formalized racial
discrimination was fading away, thanks to civil-rights reforms, the growing welfare class raised the specter of unresolvable racial inequality.

Did welfare *cause* urban disarray? AFDC originally covered only
single-parent, not two-parent, families, on the argument that the father,
if present, should be supporting the family. This restriction seemed to
generate an incentive for fathers to abandon their families in order to
qualify them for aid. To some observers it also seemed that one reason
work effort was low on welfare was that anything a welfare mother
earned would be deducted from her grant.

To liberal reformers, these problems could be cured by changing the
incentives in welfare. In order to reduce family breakup, coverage should
be extended to two-parent as well as single-parent families. To promote
employment, recipients should be given an incentive to work by being

allowed to keep at least part of their earnings. On such reasoning, Congress in 1961 allowed (but did not require) states to cover two-parent families in AFDC, provided the father was unemployed, and in 1967 it instituted a mild work incentive. Both features were included in the comprehensive reform schemes proposed by Presidents Nixon and Carter. Along with other proposals, these plans would have guaranteed an income to all Americans.

Unfortunately, however, liberal reforms did nothing to reduce dependency. Covering intact families did not stem the tide of illegitimacy in the ghetto, nor did work incentives raise work levels. Instead, the new rules themselves became a factor in the welfare boom, as they made eligible for aid many families who previously had incomes too high for welfare. Partly on these grounds, many in government eventually lost patience with liberal reform; the Nixon and Carter plans were both defeated in Congress.

Workfare: The Conservative Approach to Welfare Reform

Since the mid 1970s a more conservative brand of welfare reform has taken hold. This approach regards the abuses in welfare as moral problems, not just as technicalities, and it applies to them stronger medicine than incentives. In the last ten years, Congress has become much tougher about requiring state AFDC programs to reduce waste and fraud, and to make fathers who abandon families help pay the cost of supporting them. In 1981, the Reagan administration cut eligibility for AFDC and revoked most of the work incentives granted in 1967. Also in 1981, Congress allowed states to experiment more widely with work programs of their own; for the first time workfare was permitted—requiring the employable to "work off" their AFDC grants in unpaid jobs in local government agencies.

Since then, new work programs have proliferated at the state and local level, although the definition of workfare has expanded to include not just working off grants but education or training for work as well. Evaluations have made the new programs look reasonably successful.

Cartoon by Steve Kelley. Reprinted by permission, Steve Kelley, *The San Diego Union.*

They seem to raise earnings and reduce dependency somewhat, and at little or no net cost to the government since the expense of the new services is defrayed by savings in welfare as recipients go to work.

The current reform debate in Washington is mostly about how *federal* policy-makers should respond. The main proposals are to spend more on child care and training services in work programs, and to institute more definite requirements that employable clients participate in these programs. Essentially, the first has become the liberal, the second the conservative, meaning of welfare reform.

Research Reveals Welfare Problems

There are, to be sure, still those on the Left who attribute the vogue for workfare to the turning of the political climate: the nation, they say, is simply more conservative—i.e., stingy—than in the age of liberal reform plans. But that is a superficial explanation. The fact is that research has made the welfare problem look much tougher than it once did. Experts, even liberals, no longer believe that merely offering new benefits to the dependent can overcome their problems.

The earlier reform plans were promoted on the supposition that welfare recipients and poor people were not very different from other Americans. It was claimed that few were dependent or poor for long, and that the adults among them worked at levels fairly typical of the population at large. Nonwork could be attributed to high unemployment rates or other economic troubles.

Recent research confirms, however, what casual observation always suggested, that there is a long-term welfare class. About half of AFDC cases stay on the rolls more than two years, 38 percent for five years or longer. Moreover, a much lower proportion work today than did a generation ago. The "working poor," beloved of liberal reformers, have largely been lifted above the poverty line by economic growth. Of poor adults heading families in 1984, only 17 percent worked full-time, while 51 percent did not work at all; in 1959, both figures were about a third. Today, only about 5 percent of AFDC mothers—as compared with well over half of divorced or separated women in the population at large— work at a given time. Many single men who father welfare children also work erratically at best.

The trends are adverse even though the chance to work seems widely available. The argument that lack of jobs or other "barriers" prevent the poor from working is no longer credible. The nation has become heavily dependent on illegal immigrants to do "dirty" jobs that poor Americans decline. In most areas, jobs are plentiful, at least at low wages, and in the last two decades mothers have flooded to take them, despite low skills and the difficulties of securing child care. As the success of many recent Asian immigrants proves, the economic opportunities in this society are great, even for the unskilled. In failing to respond to these chances, welfare mothers and poor men are distinctly out of step.

In addition, experience and research have undercut the liberal hope that government can raise work levels by measures short of requirements. A succession of training and public-employment programs, virtually all voluntary, poured forth from Washington during the 1960s and 1970s. But, as with work incentives, none of them caused disadvantaged or dependent adults to work more consistently in the low-skilled jobs they could already get in the private sector, with or without the programs. Clients might accept the benefits eagerly, but this did not mean they worked more steadily thereafter.

The reason for low work effort is seldom that the poor lack opportunities, nor is it that they do not want to work in principle. While some reject low-paid work as too menial, more simply lack confidence. They hope to work, but they do not feel they can succeed at it. Nor, under current policy, do they usually have to try.

Lacking confidence, the seriously poor do not respond to economic incentives in the "rational" way that liberal reformers presumed. How, then, to overcome their *passivity*? That is the great question in antipoverty policy today. Increasingly, the solution seems to lie with public authority. To the extent that the new work programs are successful, it is probably because they make more employable recipients take work seriously than did any predecessor programs. Just as Americans accept the duty to pay taxes, yet need the IRS to remind them, so many poor adults need to have their aspiration to work reinforced by obligation.

Books Shed Little Light on the Problem

A number of books have appeared on the welfare problem recently, but they hardly reflect an adequate grasp of these realities. Most of the authors, whether on the Left or the Right, treat the long-term poor abstractly, and few offer practical policies for raising work levels.

Such predispositions are most evident among hard-line radicals, those most disposed to blame poverty and dependency on "society." Fred Block, Richard A. Cloward, Barbara Ehrenreich, and Frances Fox Piven, in *The Mean Season: The Attack on the Welfare State,* shed little light on the welfare problem, but their book helps explain why the Left has lost much of the influence on social policy it once had.

Piven and Cloward are well known for their radical interpretation of welfare. In *Regulating the Poor* and other works, they have contended that the purpose of welfare is not the promotion of a common humanity but appeasing unrest and regulating the labor supply according to the needs of the business cycle. Allegedly, welfare supports poor adults when there are no jobs for them, then withdraws aid when business needs them to perform menial labor. The current book concedes that benefit programs inevitably reduce work effort among the poor, but the authors see this as a plus, for it strengthens the "bargaining position of working people" against business. Rather than having to do just any "dirty" work offered to them, they can hold out for jobs with decent pay, and for conditions compatible with child-care responsibilities.

Cloward was one of the thinkers behind the original antipoverty program of the 1960s, which emphasized the claims rather than the responsibilities of the poor. He and Piven have also asserted that gains in social policy come not when the poor organize as an interest group but when they threaten the system with disorder. This theory did much to inspire the welfare-rights movement of the later 1960s, which mobilized militant welfare mothers to demand extra benefits.

As other historians have recognized, the Piven-Cloward interpretation is a caricature of the motives, often well-meaning, that have inspired American welfare policy. But in the 1960s and 1970s it was widely believed. It did much to make federal social planners feel guilty about the past. It entrenched the view that welfare should be an entitlement, the giving of benefits without asking anything in return. Like an angel with a flaming sword, that conviction prevented federal policymakers from even discussing the behavorial problems that plagued the ghetto.

Since the late 1970s, however, the atmosphere has been transformed. When Ronald Reagan cut welfare and many other social programs, hardly a dog barked. Welfare recipients were inactive, as was organized labor, which had mobilized effectively for the social reforms of the 1930s and 1960s. Even the wholesale loss of unionized factory jobs to foreign

66

competition has not provoked anything like the mass movement of the poor and unemployed that Piven and Cloward say must be the basis for social change.

The tone of *The Mean Season,* accordingly, is defensive, bemoaning the cuts but helpless to do much about them. The authors ridicule Charles Murray and other conservative theorists who have provided the arguments for the Reagan assault, but they admit that they have lost the intellectual initiative to the Right. The same defeatism is evident in other recent tracts from the Left, such as *The New American Poverty* (1984) by Michael Harrington, another progenitor of the War on Poverty, and Michael Katz's *In the Shadow of the Poorhouse* (1986).

Liberal Reformers Have Lost Their Authority

Why is no one listening to the Left any more? The reason has to do with more than the shifting of the political winds. The best-known radicals in social policy have also lost authority because they are no longer doing much research.

Harrington's book is an essay written about other people's research; *The Mean Season* is much the same.* These authors have collected no fresh data about the welfare problem, and in an age when most social-policy analysis is highly quantitative, that is disqualifying. A purely literary Left can no longer claim the influence it once did on issues of social policy.

But the fundamental problem with the Left's analysis is that it is no longer persuasive. These authors write out of a progressive tradition, stretching back to the origins of democratic politics, that interprets social reform as a mass struggle for equality, in which "the people," defined ever more broadly, organize to demand greater social standing from the rich and powerful. "The people" want to get ahead on their own, but also and above all they want government to protect them from the marketplace. They want "free" services, such as education and health, regulation of wages and working conditions, and welfare, pensions, and other benefits for those who cannot support themselves.

In any democratic society, that is a compelling vision. But unfortunately the last reforms that could be called progressive in this sense were the civil-rights acts of the 1960s. The last major social program serving a broad public was Medicare, which finances health care for the aged, enacted in 1965. Since then, federal social programming has been driven by concern for less inclusive groups, especially disadvantaged

---

*Piven and Cloward, in the chapters written by them, crib numbers and studies from my own *Beyond Entitlement* and other secondary sources. Fred Block's chapter on economic policy is the only one that seems based on the author's own studies.

minorities and the underclass. These groups may be needy, but they are too disordered to demand change on their own behalf. It has been provided for them, but largely at the behest of government planners, not in response to pressure from below. And when Reagan cut these programs, he did so mainly because they were ineffective, not, as *The Mean Season* suggests, as part of some generalized offensive by business against "the people."

The Mean Season Rationalizes Dependency

The authors of *The Mean Season* hark back to a vanished society in which the underdogs were personally competent, yet lacked opportunity. They complain that current opponents of welfare do not give enough credit to "the efforts of the unemployed" in the 1930s and of the "black protesters" of the 1960s. To cast our current social problem in such terms is nostalgic. Today's long-term poor and dependent seldom make such "efforts," nor do they display the discipline of the civil-rights marchers. They are seldom "working people" forced to rely on welfare as a form of temporary unemployment insurance until the right job comes along; in fact, they rarely work consistently at all. Mass-based reform is possible on behalf of the competent poor, but not on behalf of the passive poor, who do little to help themselves.

One might suppose the radical authors would support firm measures to transform inert recipients of welfare into workers who would have more capacity to press for change. But *The Mean Season* opposes workfare as just another conservative device to restrict access to aid. The authors are no longer pursuing the Left's traditional goal of equality. They are simply rationalizing dependency.

A glimmer of positive thinking occurs only in Barbara Ehrenreich's chapter, which challenges radicals to offer an "alternative vision" to conservatism, one based on the "republican values of active citizenship." But what could such citizenship mean if it does not, first of all, expect the dependent to do more to help themselves? Those who merely make demands on others are not fully citizens. In eschewing that conclusion, *The Mean Season* offers no solutions to the social problem, and expresses a radicalism no longer worthy of the name.

Case Study on Work Programs: Massachusetts' Employment and Training (ET) Choices Program

Overview: Work Programs on the State Level

Employment-related programs for applicants and recipients of Aid to Families with Dependent Children (AFDC) benefits were begun as a result of 1981 legislative changes permitting state AFDC agencies to operate work programs for their recipients. Much of the current interest in altering federal work/welfare policy is based on these recent state experiences.

State AFDC agencies have tried a variety of approaches, including (1) Work Incentive (WIN) Demonstrations, an alternative to the WIN Program, both of which are comprehensive employment and training programs; (2) Community Work Experience Programs (CWEP), a workfare approach; (3) employment search; and (4) work supplementation, where AFDC grants subsidized jobs.

Although WIN Demonstrations such as Massachusetts' Employment and Training (ET) Choices or California's Greater Avenues for Independence (GAIN) have received much publicity, little is known about the characteristics of such programs or their effectiveness. Readings 8 and 9 will focus on the Massachusetts ET program and will offer opposing viewpoints on this particular state program.

8 WORKING FOR WELFARE

THE MASSACHUSETTS MIRACLE

Michael Dukakis

Michael Dukakis presented the following testimony in his capacity as governor of Massachusetts. Governor Dukakis testified before the Senate Labor and Human Resources Committee about the success of his state's Employment and Training (ET) Choices program.

Points to Consider:

1. Why did Massachusetts' first attempt at workfare fail?
2. What has made the ET program successful?
3. How have Massachusetts' taxpayers benefited from ET?
4. In what ways does Massachusetts plan to expand the ET program?

Excerpted from testimony of Michael Dukakis before the Senate Labor and Human Resources Committee, February 3, 1987.

It is a combination—a development strategy which pays attention to regions and communities of my state that have been chronically depressed for years plus an enlightened and effective employment and training policy for people on public assistance and the unemployed and underemployed that has made the difference in Massachusetts.

I thought it would be helpful if I gave you some idea of where the Massachusetts Employment and Training (ET) Choices program came from and why we believe it has been so successful in Massachusetts and increasingly in other states which are using it as a model for their own programs.

The First Attempt

In my first term as governor from 1975 through 1978, I found myself and my state confronting a strange paradox. As our unemployment rate dropped from nearly 12 percent to 5 percent over that four-year period, the number of Massachusetts families on Aid to Families with Dependent Children (AFDC) went up and, try as we might, we found this phenomenon impossible to understand or to reverse. So, like most governors, I had my own fling at workfare. And, like most governors who tried workfare, I failed.

Retired involuntarily from the governor's office in 1978, I spent the next four years trying to figure out why our efforts to help welfare recipients move from public assistance to permanent employment failed. And I watched as a similar experiment by my successor also failed.

Why did I and Governor King fail? And why have similar programs across the country achieved so little success? Quite simply, because the overwhelming majority of families on welfare in this country are made up of single mothers with young children. And unless we want or expect those mothers to abandon their children for dead-end or make-work jobs which, incidentally make them ineligible for Medicaid, such programs will be doomed to failure.

ET: A Successful Program

What makes ET different from what we tried before is that it finally recognized these fundamental truths. And the program we have designed and which has been so successful deals with them in a way that says to these mothers and children: We're serious; we want to help you lift yourselves out of the hopelessness of dependency; and we're prepared to provide day care, real training for real jobs, and continued

71

AN "ET" SUCCESS STORY

A 24-year-old mother of two children, Carmen Colon had been on welfare for four years when she first heard about the ET program. She had worked in a shoe factory for minimum wage before her children were born but she had no other skills and did not complete high school.

Ms. Colon had an interest in electronics, however, so she enrolled in an ET-funded training program in Lawrence, Massachusetts.

Last summer, after completing the 17-week training program with a 95 percent average, Ms. Colon began working at EF Industries where she inspects and repairs broken computer components. Ms. Colon now earns more than twice what she received on welfare.

Excerpted from testimony of Michael Dukakis, governor of Massachusetts, before the Senate Labor and Human Resources Committee, February 3, 1987

medical benefits for up to a year after you find a job if your employer does not provide his other employees with health insurance.

We have also involved the private sector actively and enthusiastically in this effort. Training is provided, with the help of Job Training Partnership Act (JTPA) funds and the JTPA network, through non-profit training organizations. Those organizations provide the training under performance-based contracts that require them not only to train, but to place their trainees into jobs. No more training for non-existent jobs. If our contractor wants to get paid, it must place its students after it trains them.

The proof of the pudding is in the eating. Over 30,000 people on public assistance have obtained unsubsidized full- or part-time jobs through ET, and the overwhelming majority of them have been in the private sector. Some 8,000 employers have hired ET graduates, and I have been told repeatedly by these employers how pleased they are with the skills and motivation of our ET'ers.

Of the people who go off of welfare through ET, 86 percent are still off of welfare one year later. Moreover, ET has proven that we can crack the cycle of long-term welfare dependency: since the inception of the program, the number of participants on AFDC for five years or more has declined by 25 percent.

Finally, our taxpayers are benefiting from ET as well. We estimate that last year, after deducting the costs of the program, ET saved over $100

million in federal and state welfare savings and new revenues from the taxes being paid by our ET graduates.

These statistics are impressive, but they do not tell the whole story. For it is the human face of ET that so eloquently documents its success. And I can personally testify to the human dimension from personal conversations I have had with dozens and dozens of ET graduates and their employers about their new found feelings of self-worth and self-esteem—the sense of independence that comes with earning a paycheck instead of receiving a welfare check. . . .

Expanding the ET Program

Now that ET has proven so successful, we intend to expand it beyond AFDC recipients. People on general relief in Massachusetts are now enrolling in ET; homeless people are moving through training programs based on the ET model; more and more disabled and retarded citizens are demonstrating that they, too, prefer employment and a paycheck to a lifetime of dependency, and we soon expect to introduce ET-type programs into our correctional institutions as well.

Let me conclude by responding to what I suspect will be your first question, and that is: It's easy for you to say, Dukakis, because your unemployment rate last month was 3.3 percent. No wonder you're successful. What do we do in a state like West Virginia or Louisiana or Texas or Michigan where deep-seated, long-term economic problems are not providing the kinds of jobs that have made ET so successful?

My first answer is obvious. If there aren't any jobs out there, then we cannot seriously expect people to leave welfare. But I can assure you that we did not wait until unemployment was 3.3 percent before we launched ET. In fact, it was over 7 percent, and we had not even begun to experience the kind of extraordinary economic success that we are currently enjoying. So, ET can work even when unemployment is at or above the national average.

My second answer is equally obvious. A successful ET program must go hand in hand with an aggressive and effective economic development effort designed to revitalize those communities and regions of a state's economy that have fallen on hard times. And it is that combination—a development strategy which pays attention to regions and communities of my state that have been chronically depressed for years plus an enlightened and effective employment and training policy for people on public assistance and the unemployed and underemployed that has made the difference in Massachusetts.

9   WORKING FOR WELFARE

THE STUNNING FAILURE OF "ET"

Warren T. Brookes

Warren T. Brookes wrote the following article in his capacity as an editorialist for the Detroit News *and as a syndicated columnist.*

Points to Consider:

1. Describe the actual ET results.
2. Why has the New Hampshire program been successful?
3. Summarize the results of the Michigan MOST program.
4. Compare and contrast the results of work and training programs in Massachusetts, New Hampshire, and Michigan.

The results in Massachusetts are so poor as to call into question the entire ET program as a waste of taxpayer dollars, now nearly $50 million a year.

One of the issues on which congressional Democrats hope to create a record between now and 1988 is welfare reform, a euphemism for various forms of "workfare," or work and training.

So far, the model most often cited for this effort is the Employment and Training program (ET) started in September 1983 by Massachusetts Gov. Michael Dukakis, who has skillfully used ET's "successes," along with a buoyant state economy, as a jumping-off platform for a 1988 presidential candidacy.

Last year, Sen. Edward Kennedy co-sponsored with Rep. Jack Kemp a national welfare-work program modeled almost entirely on ET. It includes free day care for welfare recipients placed in jobs and continuation of Medicaid benefits where needed, along with extensive education and training provisions. A similar package will be introduced this year.

Actual ET Results Are Poor

But before Congress and the public become enthusiastic about a national ET, they ought to examine the *actual* record (as opposed to the Dukakis public-relations presentation) in Massachusetts. And they should compare that record with those in other states, and in particular Massachusetts' neighbor, New Hampshire, where a far less costly and elaborate job-outreach program to the private sector has accomplished much better results. In fact, the results in Massachusetts are so poor as to call into question the entire ET program as a waste of taxpayer dollars, now nearly $50 million a year.

At the end of September 1983, when the ET program began, the Massachusetts basic caseload of Aid to Families with Dependent Children was 86,999. Three years and more than $80 million in ET-spending later, the Massachusetts AFDC basic caseload has *risen*—to 87,460. (This followed a 26 percent reduction during 1981-83 from 121,400, under former Gov. Edward King's compulsory Work and Training program.)

At the same time, new applications for AFDC in Massachusetts' booming economy have risen 9 percent to 14,890 in the 1986 third quarter from 13,657 in the like 1983 quarter, while actual case terminations (mainly the result of people going back into the work force) have actually *fallen* 1.5 percent to 10,544 in the 1986 third period from 10,700 in the like 1983 period.

"ET": A MODEL FOR THE NATION?

*The ET program has made truly important steps toward help-
ing people on welfare move into employment but the program
still fails to lift many women and their children out of poverty.*

American Friends Service Committee, ET: A Model for the Nation?, September 1986

All of this was in an economy whose basic unemployment rate fell
more than 40 percent from 7.2 percent in September 1983 to 4.2 percent last September 1986.

As one Department of Health and Human Services official involved
in family assistance observed, "You have to wonder why any economy
like that needs a $50 million-a-year special training and placement pro-
gram. If you can't cut the basic caseload in that situation, there's
something very wrong with what you are doing."

Massachusetts Welfare Commissioner Charles Atkins said last year,
however, that "unemployment levels have never determined welfare
caseloads. With AFDC you're talking mostly about people who aren't
even in the labor force."

To a degree, Mr. Atkins is right, but his own ET data show more than
half of all Massachusetts monthly case terminations were people finding jobs on their own. And most national welfare studies show that for
the majority of AFDC clients, welfare-use periods are initiated and ter-
minated by changes in employment status.

New Hampshire's Formula for Success

What should most alarm Mr. Atkins is that in New Hampshire, Gov.
John Sununu has shown that low unemployment *can* be used as a
leverage to get private-sector employers to take on AFDC clients with
no investment in tax-financed bribes.

In the same three-year period (September 1983 to September 1986)
in which the Massachusetts welfare caseload rose 0.5 percent, New
Hampshire's already low caseload of 6,689 *fell* about 30 percent to 4,667,
and has continued to fall to less than 4,400.

More important, while entries into the New Hampshire system fell 18
percent, terminations rose nearly 5 percent, so the trend toward lower
welfare caseloads is continuing, and all this with a very modest "training and outreach" program that costs New Hampshire less than
$500,000 a year, or the equivalent of less than $8 million for
Massachusetts' much larger caseloads.

Welfare Caseloads in Three States

	September Total Cases	New Applications	— — Third Quarter — — Number Approved	Number Terminated
Massachusetts				
1983	86,999	13,657	10,162	10,700
1986	87,460	14,890	11,009	10,544
% Change	+0.5%	+9%	+8.3%	-1.5%
New Hampshire				
1983	6,689	2,281	1,465	1,478
1986	4,667	2,242	1,201	1,549
% Change	-30.2%	-1.7%	-18%	+4.8%
Michigan				
1983	195,784	59,095	29,218	27,559
1986	186,140	49,953	21,287	26,957
% Change	-5%	-14.5%	-27.1%	-2.2%

Sources: U.S. Dept. of Health and Human Services, Michigan Dept. of Social Services.

All this has been accomplished even as welfare benefits in New Hampshire were actually raised on a regular cost-of-living basis; they are now among the 12 highest in the nation.

Gov. Sununu's formula for success: "There is only one solution to welfare, and that's plenty of jobs—a state economy where unemployment is so low, employers are glad to accept even the hard-core welfare clients."

When Gov. Sununu took office, he surprised many of his conservative constituents by immediately proposing regular cost-of-living increases for AFDC clients. But he coupled this carrot with a commitment to use his office for outreach to the private sector for a maximum job-placement program.

"We knew that with the New Hampshire economy booming, and unemployment going down to 2.2 percent, we would never again have such a good opportunity to get AFDC folks into rewarding jobs. So we asked the private sector to cooperate."

Gov. Sununu also "changed the incentives" for the welfare caseworkers and their supervisors. "Instead of rewarding them for large caseloads, we told them they would be rated on how well they put these folks into jobs, and we made a commitment that even though caseloads came down we would not reduce staffing."

Gov. Sununu's program, the Family Incentive Plan (FIP), is voluntary ("we encourage participation very strongly") and principally involves tying together the federal Job Training Partnership Act (JTPA) training programs and counseling with strong placement outreach, but it includes none of the huge additional "incentives" available under ET.

"We do assure AFDC clients that they will keep their Medicaid benefits until they are fully employed with a private health-care program, but not after that," Gov. Sununu said.

By contrast, Massachusetts not only provides a $1,200 training package, but gives workers up to a year's worth of free day care, with an average annual cost per placement of nearly $2,800. In addition, ET placements get back-to-work clothing allowances, four months of free Medicaid and up to $10 a day travel allowances.

In fiscal 1986, the cost per ET placement exceeded $3,600, and that figure is expected to exceed $4,200 in fiscal 1987. Projecting this onto the U.S. caseload, it would cost at least $1.5 billion to $2.5 billion if it were replicated nationally.

Michigan Has More to Show

While Massachusetts claims to have placed nearly 40,000 AFDC clients into full-time jobs, its modestly rising AFDC caseloads and soaring new applications suggest those claims are open to question, and probably include many clients who normally would have found work on their own.

Indeed, given its much greater challenges, Michigan has much more to show for its $50 million annual MOST program, with compulsory job training and placement. During the same three-year period as above it cut its basic AFDC caseloads 5 percent, and new AFDC applications and acceptances fell about 15 percent and 27 percent respectively, for a lower-cost (for relative caseload) program that apparently is working in a state with a still relatively high (8 percent) unemployment level.

The varied experiences in these three states suggest the Presidential Task Force on Welfare Reform was right in wanting to leave this whole issue in the hands of the governors, and not in the more politically charged environment of Congress.

WHAT IS EDITORIAL BIAS?

This activity may be used as an individualized study guide for students in libraries and resource centers or as a discussion catalyst in small group and classroom discussions.

The capacity to recognize an author's point of view is an essential reading skill. The skill to read with insight and understanding involves the ability to detect different kinds of opinions or bias. Sex bias, race bias, ethnocentric bias, political bias, and religious bias are five basic kinds of opinions expressed in editorials and all literature that attempts to persuade. They are briefly defined below.

Five Kinds of Editorial Opinion or Bias

SEX BIAS—The expression of dislike for and/or feeling of superiority over the opposite sex or a particular sexual minority

RACE BIAS—The expression of dislike for and/or feeling of superiority over a racial group

ETHNOCENTRIC BIAS—The expression of a belief that one's own group, race, religion, culture, or nation is superior. Ethnocentric persons judge others by their own standards and values.

POLITICAL BIAS—The expression of political opinions and attitudes about domestic or foreign affairs

RELIGIOUS BIAS—The expression of a religious belief or attitude

---

Guidelines

1. From the readings in Chapter Two, locate five sentences that provide examples of editorial opinion or bias.

2. Write down each of the above sentences and determine what kind of bias each sentence represents. Is it *sex bias, race bias, ethnocentric bias, political bias, or religious bias?*

3. Make up one sentence statements that would be an example of each of the following: *sex bias, race bias, ethnocentric bias, political bias, and religious bias.*

4. See if you can locate five sentences that are factual statements from the readings in Chapter Two.

CHAPTER 3

WELFARE REFORM: IDEAS IN CONFLICT

10. WELFARE REFORM IS A GOOD INVESTMENT
    John Ashcroft

11. WELFARE REFORM WILL BE TOO COSTLY
    Peter B. Gemma, Jr.

12. WELFARE NEEDS TO BE REPLACED,
    NOT REFORMED
    Ronnie Blakeney

13. WORKFARE PARTICIPATION
    SHOULD BE MANDATORY
    Dorothy Kearns

14. WORKFARE PARTICIPATION
    SHOULD BE VOLUNTARY
    Patrick Conover

15. WE NEED A NATIONAL WELFARE POLICY
    John Larson

16. LET THE STATES CONDUCT
    THEIR OWN PROGRAMS
    William Kohlberg

17. THE GOVERNMENT IS RESPONSIBLE
    Thomas Harvey

18. THE INDIVIDUAL IS RESPONSIBLE
    Douglas Besharov

19. SOCIETY AND RECIPIENTS SHOULD
    SHARE RESPONSIBILITY
    Daniel Patrick Moynihan

10 WELFARE REFORM: IDEAS IN CONFLICT

WELFARE REFORM IS A GOOD INVESTMENT

John Ashcroft

John Ashcroft presented the following testimony before the Senate Sub-committee on Social Security and Family Policy. Mr. Ashcroft testified in his capacity as governor of Missouri.

Points to Consider:

1. According to the author, what is wrong with the current welfare system?
2. In what ways does education break the cycle of dependency?
3. Why should national welfare reform proposals acknowledge the importance of state and community-based reform?

Excerpted from testimony of John Ashcroft before the Senate Subcommittee on Social Security and Family Policy of the Senate Finance Committee, February 23, 1987.

Reform requires an investment, but it will be less expensive than perpetuation of welfare dependency. I firmly believe that the people of this nation expect more for their money than merely providing a subsistence to people trapped in dependency.

Restructuring our welfare system must be a top national priority. Our strategy must be to help Americans move from the dependency of welfare to the dignity of work, from poverty to productivity. We help people most when we help them to help themselves.

The Welfare System Is Old and Tired

Increasingly, the welfare system is criticized as an obstacle to independence. It has bred a web of long-term dependency that drains resources, productivity, and the human spirit. Analysts from all points on the political spectrum fault the welfare system for causing family fragmentation, erecting barriers to employment, excessive cost and, perhaps most troubling, for serious erosion in the aspirations and motivation levels of children in welfare families.

Our current welfare system has wrung the spirit of hope out of most of these families. We must re-awaken these citizens to their abilities and opportunities. We need their productive efforts.

Our welfare system has been around a long time. It's old, and it's tired, and it doesn't work. Our people who do not work are caught in a system that does not work—a system, in fact, that is devoted to not working. . . .

The Need for Education

To break the cycle of dependency, I believe our efforts must begin with education.

In Missouri, we know that previous job training programs for welfare clients have suffered because many of the recipients do not have the necessary educational levels to make them ready for training.

Teen pregnancy begets low educational achievement; low educational achievement begets unemployment and dependency. Even the most motivated welfare recipients face stiff competition in today's labor market without a diploma or GED. Inadequate education also prevents recipients from being competitive for job *training* opportunities. It is a vicious cycle that only education can break. . . .

Removing the Barriers

We must remove other barriers to independence and dignity. It is time for government to quit offering help only if working people give

A POSITIVE INVESTMENT APPROACH

I urge you to consider what a quality education, employment, and training program costs. This is the part of the program needed by those welfare recipients ready to prepare for long term self-sufficiency. Such a program would be an investment. It would be coupled with other policy actions ensuring adequate minimum supports for those not ready for or unable to work, improved entry wages, and strengthened child support enforcement. It would offer states the chance to design programs which match the needs of their population and their economies. To provide less or to talk about cost savings is to ignore the employment and training lessons of the past and the realities of life of the poor in America. We encourage a more positive investment approach. Evidence shows that such an approach can be successful and can result in economic independence for welfare families. Such an approach now would be worthy of the term "welfare reform."

Excerpted from testimony of Cynthia Marano, executive director of Wider Opportunities for Women, before the House Subcommittee on Public Assistance and Unemployment Compensation of the House Committee on Ways and Means, January 28, 1987

up and go on welfare. By expanding Medicaid coverage to low-income families we can prevent the fear of loss of medical benefits and remove an incentive to stay on welfare. We will also strengthen the enforcement of child support obligations and crack down on welfare fraud and abuse.

Our nation's most precious resource is its people. None of us can achieve our full potential until each of us is enabled to take full advantage of opportunities for personal development and productivity. No less than any of us, most people trapped in dependency want better lives for their families and children. We all want our children to recognize their gifts from God, and to make the most of those gifts. . . .

I began my remarks by noting that the current welfare system has spun a web of dependency that drains resources, productivity, and human spirit. As the welfare system currently exists, clients face a bewildering maze of bureaucracies that—although intended to help—pose a formidable barrier to employment: day care from one agency, job search from another, education and job training from yet other agencies. The same bureaucratic maze that faces our clients also faces our program administrators.

We must recognize that government—federal, state, or local—can only be a partner to other institutions in breaking the web of welfare dependency and building individual opportunity.

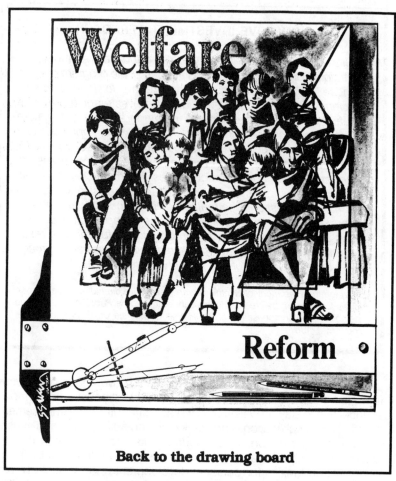

Back to the drawing board

Cartoon by David Seavey. Copyright 1987, *USA Today*. Reprinted with permission.

National Welfare Reform Requires Investment

National welfare reform proposals must acknowledge the importance of state and community-based reform. Those efforts can more successfully adapt to the unique characteristics of the fifty great states of our nation and the hundreds of local communities and neighborhoods. We need your help in changing the current rules of our welfare system that allow for little variation or experimentation. We need federal legislation providing general and system-wide waiver authority. State and local efforts to reduce welfare dependency, such as Missouri's Learnfare/Welfare-to-Work, need this flexibility to make work more rewarding than welfare. . . .

There are no simple solutions to breaking the web of welfare dependency. The key is to prevent dependency. Education and work lead to increased self-reliance and dignity. Work is always better than welfare because it ennobles people and leads to the direct opposite of dependency—independence and dignity.

Reform requires an investment, but it will be less expensive than perpetuation of welfare dependency. I firmly believe that the people of this nation expect more for their money than merely providing a subsistence to people trapped in dependency. The alternative must be to brush away the web of dependency by removing the barriers to work. Our focus must be education and jobs.

11

WELFARE REFORM: IDEAS IN CONFLICT

WELFARE REFORM WILL BE TOO COSTLY

Peter B. Gemma, Jr.

Peter B. Gemma Jr. wrote the following article in his capacity as a contributing editor of Conservative Digest. *The article originally appeared in* USA Today.

Points to Consider:

1. Why is the author skeptical about welfare reform?
2. How would the federal government generate the $5 billion or $6 billion to pay for welfare reforms?
3. Describe the issue of government-run day-care centers. Why is this reform considered controversial?

Just when we thought our meager tax reductions were safe, along come some politicians who want Washington to pay for 70 percent or more of costly, experimental welfare "reforms."

Taxpayers should beware of government bureaucrats pushing "reform." That's become a code for more expensive, more complicated, and more Washington-controlled programs.

For example, ever hear of a tax "reform" that *didn't* result in costing *more* in dollars and aggravation?

Welfare "reform" is surely needed, but the ideas being tossed around by some governors and Washington policy-makers bring two questions to mind: Can we afford it? And is it a pro-family program?

Costly Welfare "Reform"

Workfare—welfare with job responsibilities—has long been advocated by those who want incentives to ease able-bodied people off the public dole. Few will disagree with this kind of "reform."

However, that concept has been expanded into taxpayer-funded medical insurance programs, education, training and placement service, and government day-care institutions. Estimates run from $1 billion to $2 billion or more per year *extra* for these "reforms."

Add to that figure the unprecedented welfare grants proposed for low-income households where *both* parents work. The price tag on that "reform" is about $4 billion more than it costs taxpayers already.

Is anyone asking about the fathers' financial responsibilities to their welfare-dependent children?

Need to Use Caution

Just when we thought our meager tax reductions were safe, along come some politicians who want Washington to pay for 70 percent or more of costly, experimental welfare "reforms." And guess who Uncle Sam will tap for $5 billion or $6 billion of extra income to redistribute.

One of the more controversial aspects of the "reforms" being considered is a network of government-run day-care institutions. This would be in response to the proposal that every needy single mother of children age 3 and older get out of her home and into the work place.

Enticing young mothers of preschoolers out of the home is not pro-family. Common sense and compassion suggest waiting until children are at least school age before becoming latchkey kids.

Entrusting our tykes to big-brother-turned-big-momma scares me. After all, these are the same bureaucrats who run the postal "service," lose billions on Amtrak "service," and devise "simplified" tax forms.

WELFARE MANAGEMENT IS THE PROBLEM

In Weld County we consider management to be the problem—not the welfare families—the management of the programs we have and how we effectively help those families to employment. Let me list some of the programs and the different departments they are in and give you kind of a synopsis of the problem.

The Labor Department runs the jobs service under Wagner-Peyser Act, the Job Training Partnership Act, and the WIN program, or half of the WIN program. Health and Human Services runs the community work experience program or a jobs search, work supplementation, the other half of the WIN program. With HUD, we have the self-sufficiency project; with the Department of Education, we have the Carl Perkins vocational education, and so forth.

The problem becomes one of when somebody at the federal level wants to find out why we didn't get any of those people jobs—good jobs—you have to talk to 48 people and after you get done, you're totally convinced it wasn't any of them, so it must be the client.

Now, this system is also worked that way at the state level. All these departments have begot departments just like them on a smaller basis at the state level. So, if you are a governor or a member of the legislature there, you get into this conversation and you're maybe talking to 20 people now, but you've got the same problem.

It goes all the way down to the local level. You have the same diversity of programs. So, for most of our welfare recipients who are trying to get jobs, the first hurdle they have to face is applying in 58 different places to get basically the same services that are all, because of funding, very limited in nature and exactly the same, rather than putting all the funding together and having something that is a little more substantive in terms of helping folks with their problems.

Excerpted from testimony of Walter Speckman, executive director of Weld County, Colorado's Division of Human Resources, before the House Subcommittee on Public Assistance and Unemployment Compensation of the House Committee on Ways and Means, March 6, 1987

Cautious observers are asking for a practical study period at state and local levels of some of the more experimental and controversial aspects of these ''reform'' proposals.

Illustration by Stuart Leeds. © by National Review, Inc., 150 East 35th Street, New York, NY 10016. Reprinted with permission.

However, experience dictates that, unless taxpayers howl, reason and restraint have little relation with the spending habits of do-gooders.

WELFARE REFORM: IDEAS IN CONFLICT

WELFARE NEEDS TO BE REPLACED, NOT REFORMED

Ronnie Blakeney

Dr. Ronnie Blakeney presented the following testimony in her capacity as clinical director of Berkeley Academy. She has been working for welfare reform in varying capacities for 20 years.

Points to Consider:

1. Why did neighborhood round table participants want to see the welfare system replaced?
2. Describe the basic principles on which the round table participants agreed.
3. When asked how to reformulate the welfare system, what suggestions did the round table participants offer?
4. Why does the author argue in favor of local demonstrations?

Excerpted from testimony of Dr. Ronnie Blakeney before the Senate Subcommittee on Social Security and Family Policy of the Senate Committee on Finance, March 2, 1987.

From all across the nation we heard a groundswell, a mandate, a movement to not only reform, but reformulate the welfare system.

I am Dr. Ronnie Blakeney. I was a community organizer and sponsor for Welfare Rights in New York, California, and here in Washington. With my husband, Charles, I consulted with then-Governor Reagan's administration on welfare reform in California and, most recently, we advised the National Association of Neighborhoods on a 22-city study of the experiences of welfare recipients and former recipients. Today, I will summarize the findings which my husband and I describe in detail in the forthcoming volume: *Dilemmas of Dependency: A View from Across the Nation.*

Don't Reform Welfare—Replace It

In neighborhood round table discussions with over 200 people we learned that welfare is both an economic problem and a moral problem. There was a time when welfare was the means by which the government took care of those who were unable to care for themselves. But from all across the nation we heard a groundswell, a mandate, a movement to not only reform, but reformulate the welfare system. Neighborhood round table participants told us that the time has come to abandon our paternalistic system and to form a new alliance, a partnership between those who need assistance and those who provide it. This partnership must reflect a commitment to respect the dreams of those in need and reignite the determination of the poor to become self-reliant.

- We found substantial agreement on basic principles.
- We Americans believe as much in helping those in hard times as we do in the possibility of achieving dreams through opportunity and determination.
- We Americans believe in justice. We believe that our rights must be balanced with responsibilities.

Creating a Partnership

The question up for debate is: How do we create a strategy which ensures a fair balance between the partners, a balance between rights and responsibilities which is more than "a deal," in which we do more than punish those who fail to comply and reward those who cooperate? How do we create a partnership which ensures justice and compassion?

In our 22-city study, former and current welfare recipients told us that for individuals and families to climb up from dependency, people must be allowed to use their own will and determination, and appropriate

93

transitional resources and opportunities must be provided to help achieve self-reliance. In the study we asked the round table participants who should decide about the appropriate match between dreams, determination, and transitional resources. We asked how they, themselves, had succeeded in moving beyond welfare. There was substantial agreement on basic ideals.

- That there is dignity in labor;
- That family formation and maintenance is usually better than solitary struggle;
- That people need transitional resources in their efforts to move beyond dependency;
- That people want to control their own destinies to the extent that doing so is compatible with family and community life.

All across America we heard stories of courage, pride, and determination. Single mothers who organized day care cooperatives and craft cooperatives and an import-export business in Baltimore. We talked with former steelworkers who had retrained as accountants and librarians, and with former farmworkers who became secretaries, administrators, and factory workers. We talked with physically handicapped attorneys and with older Americans who created a food bank. We talked to people who could hold their heads high, and whose children could look up to them.

Reformulating the System

And when asked how they might reformulate the system consistent with their ideals, there were many different and often contradictory ideas of what would work and how to help. In some communities there was substantial agreement that absent fathers should be required to contribute child support or to perform community service. But elsewhere, there was agreement that too many non-supportive fathers were either

94

PROBLEM SOLVING...

dangerous to have around their children or former spouses, or were likely to disappear from their children's lives altogether, if their support were being monitored.

In some communities people argued that basic welfare grants should not be increased if the recipient has more children, while such notions were very controversial in other parts of the country. Some groups suggested that those who refused to participate in work or training should receive no welfare benefits; others argued that everyone was entitled to basic needs, and that children should not be allowed to suffer from their parents' failure to provide support. Still others believed that children should be removed from the home, and others thought that children should not be removed except when they were being abused.

In other words, all across the nation there was agreement on principles and disagreement about how best to achieve those goals. And that is the essence of our democracy. So I have come here today to argue for what the administration calls local demonstrations. I do so not because we don't know how to solve the problem of dependency, but because we do know.

We must restore the decision-making and consequence-determining responsibility to local communities.

We must return to a means of helping which taps the moral agency of individuals and calls upon their sense of responsibility and which ties success and failure to interpersonal and community consequences. Round table participants asked for the restoration of moral authority to individuals, families, and communities. There is a groundswell all across the nation to structure a new alliance. On their behalf, and for all of us, I ask you to let a thousand flowers bloom.

WELFARE REFORM: IDEAS IN CONFLICT

WORKFARE PARTICIPATION SHOULD BE MANDATORY

Dorothy Kearns

Dorothy Kearns presented the following testimony in her capacity as chairman of the Health and Education Steering Committee for the National Association of Counties (NACo). Ms. Kearns is also a member of NACo's Work and Welfare Reform Task Force. NACo is the only national organization representing county government in the United States.

Points to Consider:

1. In what ways has NACo supported welfare reform?
2. Why does NACo believe that the time for welfare reform is now?
3. Summarize NACo's reasons for requiring mandatory participation in employment-related programs.
4. Explain why NACo supports the use of existing employment, training, and education programs.

Excerpted from testimony of Dorothy Kearns before the House Committee on Education and Labor, April 29, 1987.

NACo supports provisions that would require clients to participate in activities designed to train and place them in jobs.

The National Association of Counties (NACo) has long been on record supporting major reforms in our national welfare system. Since 1976, NACo has urged a gradual phase-out of the Aid to Families with Dependent Children (AFDC) and food stamp programs with a goal of replacing them with a more comprehensive and productive system of services. The new system would provide jobs and training opportunities to dependent individuals who are able to work and a simplified income support program for those who are unable to work. . . .

An Idea Whose Time Has Come

NACo believes that the current welfare system is much in need of reform. Rather than enabling clients to become self-sufficient, numerous and rather uncoordinated programs have come into being since 1935—programs that tend to encourage long-term dependency. Many families in the welfare system have given up hope of ever becoming independent, productive citizens. However, members of the NACo task force are convinced that most clients want to work and will work, given realistic opportunities within appropriate frameworks of support until they can achieve independence. It is the responsibility of all levels of government to see that they have realistic opportunities to lift themselves out of poverty. I have come to believe that it is only to the extent that we are able to impact welfare reform meaningfully that we will insure a strong future for our country. In order to have an ample workforce, we will increasingly need all citizens to be productive.

We all know that nothing is so powerful as an idea whose time has come. All indications are that the time for welfare reform is now. We must not continue to use our scarce resources to encourage dependency. The nation's welfare system must be restructured to encourage clients to develop the job skills and motivations necessary to become self-sufficient. . . .

Required Participation

NACo supports provisions that would require clients to participate in activities designed to train and place them in jobs. All able-bodied welfare clients, including parents with no children under six months, should be required to develop with the welfare agency individualized self-sufficiency plans. Goals for education, training, life skills, job search, and employment should be contained in the plans, as well as incentives for cooperation and sanctions for non-compliance. Let me point out that we are not suggesting that all clients with children over six months should be required to work. Our intention here is to get young parents to start refocusing on their future as soon as possible. Under current law, it could be six years before they are provided job search assistance. We feel that six years would be too long to go without any assistance. The individualized plan would help them to set realistic goals and timetables for developing the job skills they need to become self-sufficient. It would serve as a two-way agreement between the client and the agency. The agency agrees to provide job training, job placement, and support services. The client agrees to cooperate with the agency and participate in activities designed to help get him or her placed in a decent job. Child care and transportation would be provided to clients with children.

Use of Existing Programs

To avoid duplication and waste, NACo supports the use of existing employment, training, and education programs to increase assistance available to welfare clients. The Job Training Partnership Act (JTPA), for example, could be used. If JTPA is used, federal funds must be increased to support the additional clients. We would also recommend different performance standards for welfare clients. Standards should be set for client outcomes only after realistic expectations are established based on client experience in the program.

State and Local Flexibility

States and localities must retain the flexibility to design their programs to meet the needs of their local residents. . . . State and local officials are in the best position of determining those in our communities who are most in need.

WELFARE REFORM: IDEAS IN CONFLICT

WORKFARE PARTICIPATION SHOULD BE VOLUNTARY

Patrick Conover

Patrick Conover presented the following testimony in his capacity as policy advocate for the Office for Church in Society, United Church of Christ.

Points to Consider:

1. Explain why the author believes that mandatory requirements show "a sexist lack of appreciation" for the caring of children.
2. Why does the author say that mandatory participation "is the wrong answer to the wrong problem"?
3. What percentage of eligible welfare recipients are served by JTPA? How would this fact affect mandatory participation?
4. Would mandatory requirements motivate welfare recipients who suffer from low motivation? Why or why not?

Excerpted from testimony of Patrick Conover before the House Subcommittee on Public Assistance and Unemployment Compensation of the House Committee on Ways and Means, March 11, 1987.

Some academics and some political leaders may sup-
port mandatory requirements, but the churches are not
taking this position, and neither are organizations in
which the poor are constituents.

I am pleased to have the opportunity to testify before this committee on the question of whether welfare recipients should be forced to participate in education, training, or employment-related programs as a condition to receiving benefits. Some are saying publicly that a consensus of liberals and conservatives is forming in favor of mandating participation in such programs.

Churches Do Not Favor Mandatory Participation

Some academics and some political leaders may support mandatory requirements, but the churches are not taking this position, and neither are organizations in which the poor are constituents. I would also point out that there is opposition from some business and labor groups on this point.

The movement to coerce welfare recipients to participate in education, training, or employment-related programs, represented by such spokesmen as Charles Murray and Lawrence Mead, is value driven. Thus, the fact that the churches do not favor mandatory participation should be given strong consideration, since it was the values of the church which helped to create the welfare system in the first place.

I will summarize ten reasons to oppose requiring mandatory participation. They challenge the values, theory, evidence, and practicality upon which the proposal to mandate participation is based. . . .

Ten Reasons to Oppose Mandatory Requirements

One, work as a means to meeting the financial needs of persons and families; work as a means of self-realization and of expressing one's gifts and callings; work as a means of contributing to society; and work as a means of expressing spiritual caring for the created world is a very high value. But work is not the same as employment. Mandatory requirements fail to value the work of caring for children and other dependents and restrict the choices of parents to contribute to the society by work in the sociological, if not economic, sense. They show a sexist lack of appreciation for what has traditionally been derogated as women's work, but which many are beginning to realize is a crucial investment in the future well-being of us all.

The need for good parenting is all the more pressing when it is remembered that many single parents are trying to raise children under very difficult and threatening circumstances, with children who are

VOLUNTARY PARTICIPATION IS BETTER

The American Federation of State and County Municipal Employees (AFSCME) opposes mandatory work requirements. Voluntary participation is better for several reasons.

First, success is more likely if we start out by doing a good job with a manageable number of motivated volunteers. A voluntary program can allow and challenge the states to strive for excellence instead of forcing them to focus on how to meet a legal require- ment to serve all or a certain percentage of the eligible popula- tion with what is likely to be limited funding. A successful pro- gram, in turn, will attract more than enough volunteers as well as political support for program expansion. That is the lesson of ET in Massachusetts and Head Start at the federal level.

Second, a mandatory participation requirement for mothers of young children can end up hurting the children the most. Even though many women with children work, it is not easy to juggle parental and job responsibilities. The fragility of child care ar- rangements, frequent early childhood illnesses, and unsym- pathetic employers can put a mother in the untenable position of choosing between economic security and the well-being of her children. Welfare dependent families are especially vulnerable dur- ing such times because they do not have the resources to fall back on that better-off families have. A mandatory rule could well push these mothers into choices that are detrimental to their children's interests.

Excerpted from testimony of Gerald McEntee, president of AFSCME, before the Senate Subcommittee on Social Security and Family Policy of the Senate Com- mittee on Finance, February 23, 1987

statistically more likely to have extra levels of health and educational needs.

Many single parents, mostly women, are working now under trying conditions for low pay, even when they have very young children. The need is not so much to motivate workforce participation as to protect the option for those for whom the good reasons not to work are most pressing.

Two, mandatory requirements are intrinsically unfair to that propor- tion of the poor who receive welfare benefits. It is not the poor who created high unemployment and high underemployment. They have not controlled the economic and political forces which have caused the value of the minimum wage to fall, which have exported jobs

Illustration by Geoffrey Moss. © 1984, Washington Post Writers Group. Reprinted with permission.

overseas, which have exploited the work of women and minorities, and which have shut previously open doors to opportunity.

If we listen to the cries of the poor, not just because of sympathy or guilt, but because they are the ones carrying a very expensive lesson about how our society is functioning, then we will direct attention back toward investing in the human resources which have made this country great.

Three, welfare does not cause dependency in any psychological or cultural sense. The myth that welfare causes dependency flows from the thinking of writers such as Lawrence Mead and Charles Murray and is not based on scientific research. Their research attacked the effectiveness of some antipoverty programs. Then, as experts, they declared that welfare causes dependency without offering any evidence for their assertion. . . .

Four, mandatory participation of welfare recipients in education, training, and employment-related programs is the wrong answer to the wrong problem. The problem is poverty. Education, training, and employment-related programs are antipoverty tools and deserve to be designed on their own intrinsic principles and fit to local circumstances. They should be directed by leaders and agencies with skills and orientation to fighting poverty and not made into a derivation of agencies with a very different purpose.

Five, it is unfair to make programs mandatory when the resources and opportunity are not available to meet the mandate. The amounts of resources which would be available on the most optimistic proposals currently afloat are minuscule compared to the level of need. Consider that the Job Training Partnership Act (JTPA), the largest program in this area, serves only 7 percent of those eligible and has been cut sharply in the 1980s. Consider that the average cost of child care is about $3,000 per year per child, and often for poor quality care. No one has costed out what it would take to strengthen departments of social services so that they could deliver quality case management, one-stop shopping, and comprehensive information and referral. Who has addressed the cost of quality supervision to make public service jobs worthwhile?

Six, given the low level of resources available for education, training, and employment-related programs, it is even more important that such resources be used well. Evaluation research has shown that the programs which have produced good results, such as some Job Corps programs, have been the most comprehensive and expensive programs. This argues for serving a smaller proportion of those in need but doing the job well.

Mandatory requirements would be a strong force for providing something light for everyone, and it is just such light programs which have been shown to be a waste of government money. The presumption that participation in programs should be made mandatory because of presumed low motivation—that is, laziness—is not only scientifically unfounded, as shown above; it is an expression of the stigmatization of welfare recipients which is at once unfair and a big social burden on those who take our help. To legitimize such unfair stigmatization with the force of statute would only make this problem worse.

Seven, to the extent that there are some individuals who are receiving welfare benefits who suffer from low motivation, making participation in programs mandatory is the worst way to overcome any problems. Mandatory programs externalize expectations as one more pressure to push against, while voluntary programs internalize expectations and build a sense of individual responsibility. This insight underlies both democracy and capitalism, two of the cornerstones of our nation. Why turn away from the strengths upon which this nation was built?

Eight, just as education, training, and employment-related programs should be developed in terms of their own levels of need and their intrinsic principles of effective delivery, so should services such as health care, child and dependent care. For example, child care programs should be developed to serve the needs of children and the family needs of working parents, with priority given to the children and families most in need.

Nine, there is increasing attention to the family dynamics of poverty and welfare, particularly to financial and other contributions from non-custodial parents. Directing opportunities to noncustodial parents who are supporting their children, or willing to, is an investment in long-term child support, and probably, to an improvement in family dynamics. Programs should also help sustain family unity when both parents are unemployed by not forcing a divorce so that suffering children can receive benefits.

Ten, focusing on that portion of those on welfare who could be enabled or driven into employment distracts attention from the most basic welfare problem which needs reform; that is, getting adequate resources to those in greatest need. Mandating requirements does not change the crushing realities. What does change this reality is a change in the mix of opportunity, benefits, and services.

Summary

No one should expect miracles under the current difficult situation we face. What the poor can hope for is that available resources will be used as fairly, effectively, and humanely as possible and that available political attention will be directed to making things better as rapidly as possible.

15 WELFARE REFORM: IDEAS IN CONFLICT

WE NEED A NATIONAL WELFARE POLICY

John Larson

John Larson presented the following testimony before the Senate Sub-committee on Social Security and Family Policy. He testified in his capacity as President Pro Tempore of the Connecticut State Senate.

Points to Consider:

1. Name the only Western democracy that does not have a national policy to focus on the needs of the family.
2. Why does the author believe that it is necessary to rethink and reshape family services in the United States?
3. If we do not move beyond welfare, how many children being born today will be on AFDC before reaching maturity?
4. Describe what the author refers to as the "family living standard."

Excerpted from testimony of John Larson before the Senate Subcommittee on Social Security and Family Policy of the Senate Committee on Finance, February 23, 1987.

We need a federal policy that will reinforce the family and one that can be incorporated into our national fiber both financially and philosophically.

I am very honored to be here today to testify on work and welfare from a state legislator's perspective and to represent the National Conference of State Legislatures. I congratulate Senator Moynihan and other members of the Subcommittee on Social Security and Family Policy for their foresight in attempting to frame a national policy that will address not only work and welfare but many of the other interrelated concerns which are contributing to the deterioration of the American family. . . .

We Need a Federal Policy

While we have been concentrating on promoting a new family agenda for the state of Connecticut, I believe that these issues have national significance and can be useful in structuring a national model to combat poverty and strengthen the family.

It is really distressing to note that we are the only Western democracy that does not have a national policy that focuses on the needs of the family. We need a federal policy that will reinforce the family and one that can be incorporated into our national fiber both financially and philosophically. We must start supporting programs that benefit and uplift the family as a unit. Our vision for the future of this nation must actively account for the concerns of family and we must put forward public policy that nurtures this primary institution. Without concern for our families, we will be unable to sustain a productive climate for the nation's future and in turn our economic and social environments will continue to deteriorate.

In Connecticut I have introduced a new family agenda, which will require passage of more than 30 bills to enact completely. This is a first-time effort to assess and address a complete and balanced range of family issues including day care, parental-medical leave, accessibility to health care services, housing and job training and placement. This program's impact spans several legislative committees and state agencies.

Redefining Family Services

I know that you are aware of the remarkable trends in our country. With more children than ever being raised in households steered by one working parent or by one parent on AFDC, we have a responsibility to rethink and reshape family services. While you are addressing the plight of the welfare recipient, you know that there are millions of women who comprise the working poor and are often in and out of the welfare

A STRENGTHENED FEDERAL ROLE

The federal government should maintain a strong presence, set-ting minimum benefit standards, providing adequate resources for effective programs, and supporting appropriate and effective state and local initiatives.

This principle stresses the tremendous importance of federal leadership in serving the needs of the poor. Certainly the federal government cannot and should not provide for all needs. But if history is any guide, a strengthened federal role is the surest possi-ble way to have immediate positive impact on poverty in this country.

Excerpted from testimony of Robert Fersh, executive director of Food Research and Action Center, before the House Subcommittee on Public Assistance and Unemployment Compensation of the House Committee on Ways and Means, January 28, 1987

system. Even in a rich state like Connecticut we find that children are really suffering. "Young children in Connecticut are twice as likely as adults to live in poverty. One in 15 adults in our state lives below the poverty level. One in seven children under six years of age lives below the poverty level," according to *Growing Up at Risk in Connecticut,* a collaborative project of The Connecticut Association for Human Serv-ices and The Junior League of Hartford. This signals that we may be sacrificing our children's well-being, and future generations may not be even as well off as we have been.

While we may not agree on all of the reasons why women and children find themselves in poverty, we can certainly concur that day care should be an integral part of a national policy on the family as should employment and training. We all know that American society has been forced to redefine what constitutes a family—and that is not yet clear. We have learned that families come in a variety of forms and that these families should be strengthened, supported, and valued equally. But one thing that is clear is that children who grow up in a stressful environment, with inadequate nurturing and attention, will not have a very bright future. In Connecticut alone, 40 percent of the teenage inmates in the Connecticut Department of Corrections have not received more than a ninth grade education. Kids need to get a good start. And one way to insure that kids get a good start is to establish a national policy that reflects a commitment to strengthen our working families. . . .

Cartoon by William Sanders. Reprinted with special permission of NAS, Inc.

A National Dilemma

Again, on behalf of the Senate of the State of Connecticut, I applaud your Subcommittee's efforts. While the *New York Times* has quoted Senator Moynihan as saying, "unless we move beyond welfare, we can now assume that some one-third of children being born today will be on AFDC before reaching maturity," I know that you have hope. We do not want that to happen and it is obvious that this Subcommittee is committed to find ways to solve this national dilemma because you are devoting your precious time and energy to a problem that really affects us all, even if we are not poor and have never been on welfare.

Since I have been an educator and an insurance agent, I can relate to both the economic and human concerns associated with welfare reform/replacement. While I represent a wealthy state, we have three of the nation's poorest cities and I want to see these cities and their people thrive and grow.

The Family Living Standard

In conclusion, I want *to address the family living standard* that Commissioner Heintz outlined in his recent report. American families need an economic floor to stand on, a level of living beneath which we as a society will not permit them to fall. This is our responsibility as the wealthiest nation on earth, and while we will no doubt encounter controversy as we struggle to arrive at a consensus on how this will be achieved, we must agree at least that a standard must be set. I agree that support services must be in place to prepare individuals to move to self-sufficiency and to take advantage of a comprehensive social policy, such as the family living standard.

The Connecticut family agenda will attempt to hold up the family until we replace or modify our existing system. Doubtless, there will be increased debate over a family living standard as there was in the early 1970s. However, we do need to establish a cash assistance plan for families and eliminate welfare programs that often do not promote dignity, encourage people to work, or provide a subsistence wage. We should also consider increasing the minimum wage. I believe that there will be public support to bring a family income up to a minimum standard of living, if parental support payments and earnings still leave a family with insufficient resources and in poverty.

I believe that a family living standard should reflect the basic living costs in a specific geographic area. It has been proposed that families with children will receive cash assistance in the form of a family living standard supplement based on the difference between the standard and a family's income, including wages, child support, and any other stipend, including housing assistance. Since I know that this Subcommittee is well-versed in this concept, I will conclude my remarks by stating that I feel this policy has considerable merit and will most probably be advantageous in the long run to both federal and state governments.

Conclusion

Again, I thank you for your kindness in allowing me to address this Subcommittee. We are optimistic in Connecticut. We have had some successes and we are fortunate to be involved in commenting on the future of federal policy. We share your concerns for the less fortunate who have hopes and dreams like the rest of us. Helping people is the most important thing those of us who serve in the State Capitol are charged to do. Typically, many of the issues I have addressed in my family-and-the-workplace package have traditionally been brought to the Legislature in a piece-meal fashion. I believe that our families deserve a more thoughtful approach—an approach that takes into account currently existing services offered by state agencies and adjusts them to address existing concerns. I believe you are doing this in a comprehensive way on the federal level and I applaud your efforts. ". . . Many of the things we need can wait. The child cannot. . ." (Adapted from a poem by Gabriela Mistral.)

WELFARE REFORM: IDEAS IN CONFLICT

LET THE STATES CONDUCT THEIR OWN PROGRAMS

William Kohlberg

William Kohlberg presented the following testimony in his capacity as president of the National Alliance of Business. According to Mr. Kohlberg, the Alliance has worked to promote job and training opportunities for the economically disadvantaged for 19 years.

Points to Consider:

1. Why does the author believe states should have the freedom and money to continue their welfare-to-work initiatives?
2. Describe the partnership structures involved in coordinating state programs.
3. Explain why the author favors local community coordination of welfare-to-work proposals.
4. Summarize the author's concluding observations.

Excerpted from testimony of William Kohlberg before the House Committee on Education and Labor, April 30, 1987.

The most important contribution the federal government can make to improve the transition from welfare to work is to give the states the freedom and the "seed money" to continue their efforts.

I welcome this opportunity to discuss what the National Alliance of Business believes is the critical component of welfare reform—the provision of employment, education, and support services to welfare recipients to prepare for competitive employment in the private sector. Today, there is nearly universal agreement that such activities are an indispensable part of any strategy to overhaul this nation's welfare policies. We believe that this rare political consensus can provide a solid basis for new welfare-to-work legislation to replace the Work Incentive (WIN) program.

This Committee is in a unique position to fashion a welfare-to-work program that is both internally consistent and easily coordinated with existing employment and training activities. The new legislation should consolidate the various federal welfare-to-work pieces into one single program that is flexible in design and simple in administration.

Allow States the Freedom to Conduct Programs

New welfare-to-work initiatives being established in a few key states provide a good foundation on which to reshape federal policy. For a number of years, the WIN program has been the main tool used by states to provide a comprehensive mix of job search and training activities to welfare recipients. In recent years, the WIN grant money has played a critical role in leveraging additional financing from state legislatures to make more imaginative programming possible. New federal legislation should build on successful state experiments conducted over the past several years, incorporate their lessons, as well as positive lessons from other employment and training programs, and draw on research findings that suggest promising new approaches to solving old problems.

We must be careful not to take a heavy-handed approach that could stifle the creative efforts being made by individual states. The most important contribution the federal government can make to improve the transition from welfare to work is to give the states the freedom and the "seed money" to continue their efforts. . . .

Partnership Structures

One of the largest unresolved issues concerning a new welfare-to-work program is its administrative structure. States that are operating effective welfare-to-work programs currently employ a wide variety of administrative structures.

AN "ET" GRADUATE SPEAKS

My name is Dawn Lawson, and I am 29. I have a 10-year-old son, Brian.

I was on welfare for almost seven years. When my son was ready to go to school, they told me I would have to try to find some type of work. So right before he started I took a job as a nurse's aide. I was not earning very much money, and I was still getting Medicaid and food stamps and housing. I was getting everything except for a check.

I was very unhappy in the job, and I went back to the welfare office, and they said there was a position open in a word processing course through the ET program. It seemed so interesting, and the thing that I really was excited about was that I would have a marketable skill in a short time, and I could break away from welfare permanently.

I was in the training program for about three or four months, and Norton Company, which I work for now, was backing this program up. They asked me if I wanted to try out an internship program and to use the skills that I was learning. And after a short time, they asked me if I wanted to become a full-time employee there.

It has been really nice, because I worked as a word processor for three years, and last month I got promoted to an international salary specialist, which deals with handling all the overseas executives' pay and their taxes.

ET has opened doors for me that would never have been opened before. Even in just the last year, I started my own word processing business at home, and I do resumes. So many things have changed for me. I have moved out of public housing, and I have taken my son on trips. I have been able to put him into a decent school. I bought a car. Just so many things keep changing and getting better and better. And I do owe it to ET for that.

Excerpted from testimony of Dawn Lawson, a graduate of Massachusetts' ET Choices program, before the Senate Committee on Labor and Human Resources, February 3, 1987

Over the past several years, individual states have been struggling to reshape their service delivery systems to meet the training needs of welfare recipients. A major thrust has been the coordination, and in some cases integration, of related human resource development functions within the state, often achieved through a state-level strategic plan-

ning process that addresses a broad spectrum of state programs. The key players have been the governors, who are in a unique position to fashion a rational system through their authority over state administrative agencies. Consequently, we would prefer to leave discretion with the governors to designate the appropriate state agency to administer their program.

In addition to the governors, and acting under their authority, the existing state job training coordinating councils, authorized under the Job Training Partnership Act, can be a valuable tool to promote effective strategic planning and program coordination at the state level. These councils bring together key actors within the state to advise the governor on state employment and training needs. The council is responsible for preparing a state "coordination and special services plan" to guide the coordination of related state programs such as education, public assistance, employment service, rehabilitation for the handicapped, and economic development. The state council is also required under current law to review the plans of all state agencies providing employment and training services and to make recommendations to the governor, state agencies, and the state legislature for improvements. . . .

Local Coordination

We are concerned that none of the welfare-to-work proposals contain any requirements for local planning to take into account variations in economic conditions, employer and client characteristics, and resource availability. The real center of gravity for welfare employment and training activities is in the local communities. Welfare recipients enter the system when they apply for benefits at local offices, and from there must be referred to appropriate education, training, or supportive services offered in that community. Local planning should be required that takes into account the different circumstances in each community and addresses how existing resources will be utilized.

The local planning process offers a means to help coordinate related activities within the community and to streamline the delivery of needed services. Since the education, training, and support services needed by welfare recipients are presently being provided in many communities, using new program funds to provide a separate system of facilities or services just for welfare recipients would lead to unnecessary duplication of effort and waste of scarce public resources.

The new legislation should require local welfare-to-work agencies to submit the job training and work preparation components of their local plans to appropriate local elected officials and private industry councils for review and comment. We would also recommend that the local agency(ies) operating the welfare-to-work program be required to submit necessary information to the private industry councils regularly on job training and work preparation activities so that the councils can provide valuable oversight to the program.

The private industry councils are evolving into "boards of directors" for employment and training programs in local communities. Many states already require welfare agency representation on the councils. . . . In some areas, the private industry councils have already broadened the scope of their activities to include participation in state welfare-to-work initiatives. For example, the Massachusetts "ET Choices" program makes extensive use of local private industry councils. Since the private industry councils are required by law to plan and oversee programs for welfare recipients, their involvement in this new welfare-to-work program would be an appropriate addition to their existing statutory responsibilities. . . .

Concluding Observations

We are concerned that the opportunity for establishing such a welfare-to-work program could be lost by forcing political agreement where there is none. While there is broad agreement on the need for welfare reform, many of the proposals that have been advanced remain the subject of considerable controversy. The only reform that appears to command universal agreement is the expansion of education, employment, and related support services to welfare recipients. In the event the proposed work program gets mired in debate over the non-work aspects of welfare reform, and passage appears unlikely, we would urge the Committee to consider pursuing an alternative strategy that separates the work program from the larger package.

Finally, we would recommend the continuation of funding and authority necessary for the stability of ongoing state initiatives until new federal legislation can become effective.

WELFARE REFORM: IDEAS IN CONFLICT

THE GOVERNMENT IS RESPONSIBLE

Thomas J. Harvey

The Reverend Thomas J. Harvey presented the following testimony in his capacity as executive director of Catholic Charities USA. He testified before the House of Representatives Subcommittee on Public Assistance and Unemployment Compensation.

Points to Consider:

1. Why does the author describe current benefit levels and the AFDC program as "an affront to the conscience"?
2. Define and/or describe the official poverty line.
3. Explain why Catholic Charities USA supports voluntary participation in work-related programs for mothers with young children.
4. What kind of assistance should the government provide to people in their transition to the workforce?

Excerpted from testimony of Reverend Thomas J. Harvey before the House Subcommittee on Public Assistance and Unemployment Compensation of the House Committee on Ways and Means, March 10, 1987.

Clearly the federal government has a necessary and basic responsibility in the income maintenance area, for this economy is a national economy, not governable by the policies of the various states.

I am pleased to be able to present the views of Catholic Charities agencies around the country not merely on ways in which we might reform our basic national welfare program, but also on the importance of doing so in a way which asserts both the compassion of the American people, and our sense of justice. We are encouraged to see the Congress focus on what can be done for our neediest citizens, especially those served by the Aid to Families with Dependent Children (AFDC) program. . . .

An Affront to the Conscience

For some 20 years we have been stymied over either how to reform welfare or how to manage costs. In the meantime the sustenance provided families in need of this assistance has declined about 40 percent in real dollars. The poorest people have become poorer even as we somehow expected to see them pull themselves up by their bootstraps. The United States has not given this population any of the benefits which have come from the tax cuts or the farm subsidies, though government has all but eliminated subsidized housing starts. Current benefit levels, and much more about the AFDC program, are an affront to the conscience.

I say this both because of the religious teachings of my church about justice in the economic order, found in the statements of the Catholic Bishops, and because it is undeniably a judgment which is shared by the other religious denominations which make up our pluralistic society. I say it, too, based on the experience of the hundreds of Catholic Charities agencies and programs around the country which are involved in providing service and advocacy for those least provided for in this society, those most hurt by lack of opportunity.

We are pleased to see a good measure of consensus reflected in most of the proposals offered by leading members of the Congress, and by other important groups in our society. It is obvious that during the past 20 years, while the Congress has been immobilized on welfare reform, a generally accepted consensus has developed on some basic values which any welfare reform ought encompass. Clearly, there is a strong consensus that we do not need an additional prolonged era of benign experiments such as the Administration's proposals would encourage. Now is the time to begin to legislate a way out of the present inhumane system to one which provides adequate support for families, assistance for families to enter the economic mainstream, and a supplement to their income if this economic system doesn't offer adequate income protection for the necessities of life.

A Genuine Federalism

The consensus we see is one which reflects a genuine "federalism" partnership between the national government and the states, not an abdication of federal responsibility. Clearly the federal government has a necessary and basic responsibility in the income maintenance area, for this economy is a national economy, not governable by the policies of the various states. There is a consensus, also, that any basic economic assistance program for families ought to be designed to help preserve the integrity of those families. There is a clear recognition that today, with an increasing percentage of mothers in the workforce, society expects the family to sustain itself by work, wherever possible. And in order to make a transition to the working world possible for some parents, there is agreement that more must be done in the way of providing education and training, and to make the transition to gainful employment economically feasible. While there does not seem to be accord on basic benefit levels, there is a good deal of recognition that our citizens have some collective responsibility to see that the lowest income citizens are not both employed and still living below the poverty line.

Illustration by Geoffrey Moss. © 1983, Washington Post Writers Group. Reprinted with permission.

Two things can be said about the official poverty line used by the government. It was, first of all, a measure of income level for a short period of time. Secondly, this poverty line has been falling rapidly over the past two decades as a percent of median income. In other words, again, those in poverty—which include, I think, everyone receiving AFDC assistance—have been getting poorer steadily, for 20 years, in relation to the rest of the population. . . .

Two-Parent Families

Even if full scale welfare reform is not completed this year, now is the time to enact a mandated program to cover two-parent families.

There is no more key principle to be asserted in improving welfare than that the program does nothing to weaken, and everything to strengthen, family life. Yet about half the states still require the absence of a parent before providing AFDC assistance. There can be no reasons for this other than a desire to cut down on government spending or poor program design. And these are not sufficient reasons to foster desertion or cheating. Other than an emphasis on work, there is no clearer consensus in this nation than that welfare ought to help families, not hurt them. Not infrequently do our Catholic Charities agencies have to provide services to both sides of a marriage rendered asunder by a program of the state. Both marriage partners suffer; the children suffer even more. Indeed society suffers.

I repeat, whatever else Congress gets time to consider this year, we urge that a two-parent family benefit be moved forward without delay.

Dependency and Work

I observed above that changing female participation in the workforce, for whatever reasons, has clearly changed the view of what the public will support through public assistance. In addition we are all aware of what has seemingly been a growing problem of dependency on welfare assistance on the part of some, rather than the expected reliance on work for a livelihood. So we support a well-crafted set of programs designed to help most adult recipients move to participation in the workforce. However, we most strongly urge participation in such programs be voluntary for mothers with small children, and any adult necessary in the home to care for a disabled child or adult. We think an exception to mandatory programs should be provided for mothers with children under six, or first-grade age. Our concern here is twofold: the enduring life-long valued nurture provided by close parenting of young children can be the most valuable investment we can encourage. Secondly, many of the children we are talking about live, we must recognize, in areas of our communities where it is the most difficult to provide for nurturing and protection.

For other adults, however, a well integrated and managed program of supplemental education, work training, and transitional assistance to active participation in the workforce, is needed on an expanded scale. I am not talking about "workfare." I am talking about eventual meaningful jobs. In Catholic Charities, we believe that it is the government's responsibility both to help people get ready to work and to see that the jobs are there if the private economy does not provide them.

We also acknowledge that we must provide assistance in the transition to the workforce, and supplementation if the only work available still leaves the family in poverty. Thus the protection of Medicaid must be available for a reasonable length of time, and to a reasonable level of income. There must be available and affordable day care. And if the only work available is at current minimum wage, for example, additional

123

financial assistance through AFDC or food stamps must be provided. And for families at a very low income, such assistance must vary by family size.

Adolescent Mothers

Among the many areas of service engaging Catholic Charities agencies is working with pregnant adolescents and their families. On the basis of our experience we believe that such teenagers should be encouraged to stay with their families, but that a requirement that they do so could in very many instances be harmful to the development of their maturity, to their siblings and parents, and to their child. This is a requirement which will save no one money in the long run, but may continue the devastation which has begun. For those teenagers whose pregnancy is the result of acting out and conflict within their family such a requirement could be devastating. For others whose families reject them there often is nowhere else to turn.

On the other hand a constructive way to encourage them to stay with their parents, if that is possible, is to make it easier for them to stay by not counting the income of the parents in determining eligibility for a benefit. Many children leave their families for no other reason than that is the only way they can get Medicaid coverage for the pregnancy and delivery, a cost their families could not otherwise bear. Such a policy is shortsighted.

Case Management

Every once in a while some magazine or newspaper screams that someone on welfare is getting or is eligible for multi-thousands of dollars of benefits through various programs. I have never found any poor person who has made it good like this, though there may be a few fraudulent recipients. What these stories do say to us is that the systems which provide assistance are complex and not well integrated. While we would assume that any reforms you undertake would integrate programs better, we would argue for the *availability* of a case management approach, especially for those recipients, who through some combination of characteristics, are needlessly dependent on public assistance.

I say this, even though I generally believe that eligibility for public assistance ought to be determined on an entitlement basis in our society, and not ultimately be dependent on utilizing casework services. Thus we do not believe that in good conscience you can cut the mother of a seven-year-old off from assistance because she won't cooperate in a work/study program, and leave only a pittance of assistance for the seven-year-old. That is a problem of protective services.

But the extensive experience of our agencies in resettling thousands and thousands of refugees, speaking no English, and with work skills largely alien to our economy, suggests there are ways of helping people negotiate the system, to facilitate negotiating the path from dependency to a life of self-sufficiency in the economy of our country.

National Responsibility

I admire the thoughtful process the governors and the American Public Welfare Association (APWA) have gone through in an effort to arrive at a consensus on welfare reform. But I believe history quite clearly tells us that there ought be a national minimum benefit. Of course state supplementation should still be encouraged. But the fact that the great majority of the states have for years had a great discrepancy between their own level of benefit and their own standard of need is clear evidence that adequacy of benefit across the nation will not be reached without a national minimum benefit. To ease the transition to such a benefit, we believe that the federal government ought to bear an increased share of the costs. Finally, it should be obvious that benefits should be indexed to inflation. If the tax system is so indexed, why not protect the poorest among us as well.

In closing let me express the earnest interest of Catholic Charities around the country in the task you have before you to lead the nation to a better way—a more compassionate way—a more just way of helping the poorest of our fellow citizens.

18

WELFARE REFORM: IDEAS IN CONFLICT

THE INDIVIDUAL IS RESPONSIBLE

Douglas Besharov

Douglas Besharov is a resident scholar at the American Enterprise Institute for Public Policy Research. He testified before a House of Representatives subcommittee on behalf of the Working Seminar on the Family and American Welfare Policy.

Points to Consider:

1. Define and/or describe behavioral dependency, as it is referred to in this reading.
2. Why does the Working Seminar approve of holding welfare recipients responsible for becoming self-sufficient?
3. How would increased emphasis on the family help overcome the behavioral dependency problem?
4. Do you agree with the Working Seminar's recommendations? Why or why not?

Excerpted from testimony of Douglas Besharov before the House Sub-committee on Public Assistance of the House Committee on Ways and Means, March 13, 1987.

Our report argues that it has been a mistake to offer welfare benefits without imposing on recipients the same obligations faced by other citizens, to try to become self-sufficient through education, work, and responsible family behavior. . . .To hold all people responsible, as befits their abilities, for acquiring those skills and competencies necessary to self-reliance is only just. And while many may need some assistance, to hold those on welfare personally responsible, too, is no more than is asked of other citizens.

Two centuries ago, a French immigrant, J. Hector St. John de Crevecoeur, wrote of the new American settler, "From involuntary idleness, servile dependence, penury, and useless labor, he has passed to toils of a very different nature, rewarded by ample subsistence." And so, for most Americans, it remains today. A resident of the United States can virtually guarantee a life free from poverty by accomplishing only three things: completing high school, staying in the labor force, and establishing a family. Such, still, are the blessings of this land.

Locked in Behavioral Dependency

Yet, a numerically small but significant group of our fellow countrymen fails to partake of this bounty. They are poor in means, but it is not their poverty that is most distressing. They often depend upon public assistance, but it is not their dependency as such that is worrisome. (The elderly and the disabled also rely on income supports, but arouse no comparable concern.) They are concentrated in large and generally prosperous cities, but it is not where they are located that really matters.

Rather, what is most important is their isolation from American society, their inability to acquire the skills and attitudes essential for functioning successfully in American life, their weakened morale and lack of self-esteem. Without these, their chances of attaining the rewards of self-reliance that constitute the birthright of all Americans are slim. They remain locked, instead, in a behavioral dependency that belies their status as American citizens.

In keeping with another national tradition, Americans of all political and philosophical persuasions have sought ways to help this group out of its plight. We have given generously of our own wealth, through both public and private channels. We have invented new methods for enveloping them in the American ethos. We have reached out and involved ourselves in their lives. We have had some successes; we have

127

SENDING THE WRONG MESSAGE

As the size of the welfare state has grown, it's clear that it is failing in its goal to eradicate poverty. In fact, it has institutionalized poverty and created what some fear is the permanent dependent underclass.

In the 1960s, social policy in the United States was changed by the Johnson administration and given the name "War on Poverty." The basic rules for getting ahead were changed and incorporated in a welfare system designed to uplift the poor. What it did, however, was to trap millions of young adults in poverty. The reasoning for the new social policy was primarily based on the notion that all social ills are the fault of society. For example, if you don't have a job, it is society's fault for not providing you with one; if you are young, unmarried and having a baby, the system is to blame; if you fail in school, it is because you're not being provided with the education you need. Therefore, it is the duty of society to set things right.

We have sent the wrong message to our young people. We have removed individual responsibility and caused them to work, study, and marry less.

Nancy Duersten, "Welfare System Creating a Generation without Responsibility," Milwaukee Journal, May 28, 1985

also had some failures. And some of what we have done may have hurt more than helped. Yet, we remain ready to try again. . . .

The Working Seminar on the Family and American Welfare Policy

In the past year, the Working Seminar on the Family and American Welfare Policy has commissioned nearly a dozen research papers, held a half-dozen meetings, and engaged in numerous informal discussions with knowledgeable observers from around the country. We have also had the benefit of reviewing the reports and conclusions of several other groups that have examined this problem from different vantage points. In our own report, entitled *A Community of Self-Reliance: The New Consensus on Family and Welfare,* we seek to distill the essence of this now considerable body of information and ideas to construct a set of principles that we believe ought to guide a new round of welfare reform.

The starting point for all of these is the recognition that low income and behavioral dependency are two quite different problems and require different remedies. Approximately 33 million Americans are considered poor, using the official Census Bureau measure. (A broader

measure, including in-kind benefits such as food stamps, would reduce this to roughly 22 million.) But no more (and probably much less) than one-third of that number (many of whom are children, living in families headed by an adult) are likely to present the kinds of problems that seriously diminish the likelihood of becoming self-reliant. For the rest, an expanding economy, improvements in income support and tax policies, and other adjustments in our current ways of helping the poor should be sufficient to enable them to participate more fully in American life, if they wish to do so.

Our report describes this new form of poverty—"behavioral dependency"—which is caused not by low income alone, but by a growing inability to cope. Many people stay dependent on welfare through their own behaviors, such as dropping out of school, having children out of wedlock, and failing to work. The traditional solution of economic growth plus income supplements is not working well enough to diminish their dependency. . . .

We therefore make a series of recommendations on how religious institutions, schools, the media, and neighborhood and professional associations can become involved in responding to the plague of dependency. At every level, those who help to shape the national ethos must help recreate our two-sided ideal of community and self-reliance.

The Concept of Obligation

There is a common idea which should serve as the basis of the efforts of all these institutions. It is the concept of obligation. No person should be involuntarily poor without others coming to his or her assistance. No able adult should be allowed voluntarily to take from the common good, without also contributing to it. Parents should be expected to support their children; children should be expected to prepare themselves for becoming self-reliant adults. The mass media, religious bodies, voluntary groups, schools, law enforcement authorities, and other institutions important in the lives of the poor should assert standards of conduct conducive to avoiding dependency and expect that they be adhered to. When obligations are not met, the consequences should be felt, except where harm might befall innocents.

In other words, the problem of behavioral dependency requires us to go beyond questions of income in order to attend to questions concerning the way people organize their lives. What is distinctive about behavioral dependency is its moral or attitudinal component. It is not enough for the makers of public policy to attend to externalities and public arrangements, without also being aware of the ways in which policy impinges—or fails to impinge—on personal and social values. Private institutions likewise have a responsibility to help shape an ethos favorable to those of the poor seeking to practice the traditional disciplines by which Americans have long bettered their own conditions and those of their families. By emphasizing obligations, society can help inculcate and reinforce the values and habits essential to escaping poverty.

Nevertheless, government policy plays a crucial role: it sets goals for citizens and incites efforts. Therefore, our report also makes major recommendations for government action. Our report argues that it has been a mistake to offer welfare benefits without imposing on recipients the same obligations faced by other citizens, to try to become self-sufficient through education, work, and responsible family behavior.

In addition, it can help restore self-respect to the poor. Often in the past, programs designed to help persons of low income have offered benefits without imposing any duties in return. This is to treat them as less than full citizens. To hold all people responsible, as befits their abilities, for acquiring those skills and competencies necessary to self-reliance is only just. And while many may need some assistance, to hold those on welfare personally responsible, too, is no more than is asked of other citizens. And much more than is expected of clients. Such a change in self-image is indispensable for reducing behavioral dependency.

Beginning with the Family

For developing a sense of personal responsibility, for transmitting social values and habits, for providing aid and comfort, no institution is as important as the family. Indeed, the problem of behavioral dependency is largely (though not entirely) one of the family. Eighty percent of the poor live in families; sixty percent live in families with children under eighteen; of the latter, half are headed by a single parent. Such families are doubly disadvantaged; they often lack earning power sufficient to make good use of the economic opportunities available to them and some are also short on the social resources necessary to instill the skills for self-reliance in their members. Misguided public policies and activities by private groups have, as well, sometimes increased more than they have lightened the burdens such families face.

Hence, the crucible for the next round of welfare reform must be the family. All our efforts should be directed toward reducing the number of single-parent families, or for those that are created, insisting that adequate support—educational and nurturing as well as financial—be maintained. To be sure, 25 years of experience have demonstrated that these goals are easier proclaimed than achieved. But it is essential to continue proclaiming them, and trying to realize them, through both public and private efforts, if the challenge of behavioral dependency is to be met.

Specific Recommendations

To that end, we offer a number of specific recommendations. They are neither earth-shattering nor unique. We do not believe there is a magic answer, a simple but as yet undiscovered solution, to the problem we face. (The closest, the foundation for all else, is economic growth, but even it is not sufficient to deal with the kind of dependency that concerns us.) Rather, we think the best hope lies in mobilizing an across-the-board effort, built on the following principles:

I. *The home environment for young children in impoverished families should be the primary location for preventing future dependency.* Parental responsibility for the support of children should be reinforced; political and administrative pressure should be brought to bear to improve the level of child support enforcement. The fathers of out-of-wedlock children should be identified through mandatory paternity findings. Voluntary associations should help young mothers through classes in child care and child education, and other efforts that bring these mothers out of isolation, in social settings that provide child-care and instruction.

131

In regard to teenage mothers, welfare policy should not confuse their legal status as parents with their physical and emotional standing, which may be less than adult. Consequently, unless there is a finding that their safety so requires, welfare benefits should not be paid to recipients under 18 living in independent households. . . .

II. *Schools should impose high standards of achievement, behavior, and responsibility on all students.* Communities should be encouraged and assisted in setting high standards for their schools, recognizing that the key factors are: strong principals, an orderly but not rigid school atmosphere, a schoolwide commitment of resources to and focus on basic skills; a highly visible expectation that every child can learn; and frequent monitoring of the performance of every student.

Fear of lawsuits claiming the violation of "student rights" has deprived some school officials of a spirit of initiative and led others to take the course of least resistance, for example by not enforcing standards of behavior that they know have been violated. Federal law should be amended so that, within appropriate limits, principals have greater good-faith discretion in setting and enforcing schoolwide standards of behavior.

Parental involvement in schooling should be increased, perhaps, by giving parents a greater measure of choice regarding which public schools their children attend. Some members of the Working Seminar favor a voucher or an open enrollment plan; others doubt the practicality of such plans. All agree in seeking ways to give poor parents more of the flexibility and freedom others already have, and to make the public schools more accountable for their performance among the poor.

III. *The rights of the poor to integrity of life, limb, and property should receive equal protection under the law.* To reduce the scourge of crime in the communities of the poor, innovative methods of policing should be introduced, court procedures tightened, and the illegal drug trade better controlled. Standards of conduct in public housing should be enforced, and volunteer efforts, such as neighborhood associations, encouraged.

IV. *Since voluntary associations have a public character and public responsibilities, they should focus their power on reducing behavioral dependency.* The mass media should help nourish a moral environment in which the habits crucial to exiting from poverty are reinforced, religious institutions should challenge the poor and empower them through spiritual determination, inner strength, and community involvement, and other voluntary groups should employ their own special skills and resources to invent new ways of coming to the aid of the poor and dependent.

V. *Welfare recipients should be required to take part in work (or time-limited training programs) as a condition of receiving benefits.* Young mothers should be required to complete high school (or its equivalent) and prepare themselves for future employment. Older mothers with previous work experience should be expected to find work in the private sector or (as a last resort) to accept assignment in the public sector. Those involved in work programs, whether staff or participants, should be expected to regard every job, even part-time and at minimum wage, as an obligation to society, as important to future work experience, and as an occasion for self-development.

VI. *The implementation of work programs should move forward cautiously and in graduated steps.* Programs should neither be massive nor designed for swift results but for steady progress in increasing the share of the employable engaged in constructive work. States and localities should have a financial incentive to reap the benefits of the savings gained by moving the dependent from passive recipiency to productive work.

VII. *Cash benefits should be transitional in nature.* After a specific time limit (such as two years), a recipient of Aid to Families with Dependent Children (AFDC) would be required, as a condition of further assistance, either to find employment or to accept a public job.

VIII. *Clear and fair sanctions should be imposed on able recipients of benefits who fail to work without good cause (such as physical or mental disability).* The vast array of rules and procedures that have grown up around access to public assistance programs—frequently as the result of judicial actions—must be critically reexamined. Some rulings seek one-sidedly to protect the rights of recipients to benefits, without giving due emphasis to the obligations that recipients have to the rest of society, including the duty to seek to become self-reliant.

IX. *The working poor should not be taxed into poverty.* State and local income taxes should be adjusted to lift their burdens on the working poor. Expansion of the Earned Income Tax Credit to offset more of the burden of federal payroll taxes should be carefully examined.

X. *In the administration of welfare, the principle of federalism should be maintained, but policies should be adjusted to emphasize state and local innovation.* State and local governments should be given great latitude to experiment with methods of reducing poverty and dependency. Federal rules and regulations should be reviewed to be sure that these do not unnecessarily complicate or limit state and local initiatives. Standards for assistance to the poor should reflect local living conditions.

These recommendations do not contain the specifics that might be required for a legislative proposal or administrative action. In our view, such details must inevitably be worked out pragmatically, through the give-and-take of the political process, where the ideal yields to the realistic. While we would be eager to discuss legislative changes with the committee, far be it for us to try to make such judgments in advance and in any case, there are already enough specific proposals, bills, and reform plans before the public that another one would only add to the confusion. It is urgent that the nation act—not lose its way in the forest of technicalities which have too often entered into discussions of welfare policy in the recent past. We hope the principles we have set forth will serve to identify the crucial issues with which all serious initiatives should deal and be a bipartisan standard by which to judge how well they are likely to work.

19 WELFARE REFORM: IDEAS IN CONFLICT

SOCIETY AND RECIPIENTS SHOULD SHARE RESPONSIBILITY

Daniel Patrick Moynihan

Senator Daniel Patrick Moynihan presented the following testimony in his capacity as Democratic chairman of the Senate Subcommittee on Social Security and Family Policy. Senator Moynihan has been credited by The Washington Post *for "jump-starting" the welfare debate and pointing liberals and conservatives in a direction that both might find comfortable.*

Points to Consider:

1. Why does Senator Moynihan believe that AFDC cannot work?
2. What does he suggest should be done with AFDC?
3. Summarize the three themes that have resulted in a bipartisan consensus. Do you agree with this emerging consensus? Why or why not?
4. Describe Senator Moynihan's proposed "social contract" between welfare recipients and the government.

Excerpted from testimony of Daniel Patrick Moynihan before the Senate Subcommittee on Social Security and Family Policy of the Senate Committee on Finance, February 2, 1987.

We are hearing a recurring theme, that of a new "social contract." A contract in which parents assume the primary financial responsibility for their children—absent parents by paying child support and custodial parents by working as much as is practicable. In exchange, the community, through temporary government assistance, will assure that children and the families raising them receive adequate income and health care.

In his State of the Union message, President Reagan said he would submit to the Congress "a new national welfare strategy." With the President interested in overhauling the family welfare system and Democratic and Republican leaders in the Congress intent on improving the lot of children and their families, we may be able to evolve a system that we do not now have.

AFDC Cannot Work

We need such a system. The American Public Welfare Association reports that one child in four is born into poverty today; one in five will grow up poor. The principal program now supporting poor children, Aid to Families with Dependent Children (AFDC), does not and cannot offer poor families the hope of becoming self-sufficient.

Of course, AFDC was never intended for this purpose. It was designed, in 1935, to tide over poor widows and orphans who were not yet entitled to receive Survivors Insurance benefits, added to the Social Security Act in 1939. Moreover, the AFDC program was never meant to respond to the social conditions of the 1980s. Neither the dramatic increase in female-headed families, nor the expectation that women would work outside the home, was anticipated 52 years ago.

This mismatch between the social expectations of a bygone era and today's social realities helps explain the precipitous decline in the value of the benefits we pay to needy children. Between 1970 and 1986, the purchasing power of AFDC benefits in the median state (in constant dollars) declined by one third—at least for the children receiving such benefits. In 1985, there were over 12 million poor children in the United States; only seven million qualified for AFDC.

We have a program that reaches less than two thirds of those who need it, a program in which benefits have been allowed to decline. This is not a program that commands political support.

Replace AFDC

That is why I suggest we replace, rather than reform, AFDC. Replace
it with a national system of child support—a system that relies first and
foremost on parents to support their children. In single-parent families,
the absent fathers (it is fathers who are absent in 90 percent of such
families) must be required to pay a portion of their income to help support their children. Mothers must help support their children by working, at least part-time, outside the home. If parental support payments
plus earnings still leave the household's income below a stipulated
minimum benefit level, we must then provide for our children with public
support.

Simply put, parents must assume primary financial responsibility for
their children. Only after both parents are doing their fair share should
public assistance be provided. The lead editorial in the *Washington Post*
of January 30, 1987 suggests that this approach may "liberate" liberals
and conservatives—allowing us, finally, to act in concert on behalf of
our children.

It is essential that we act. In 1985, 22 percent of children under age
18 were living with one parent. But 60 percent of all children born in
1985 can expect to live in a single-parent family before reaching their
18th birthdays. If we do not move beyond "welfare," one-third of our
children can expect to become AFDC recipients for some portion of
their childhoods.

Cartoon by Richard Wright. Reprinted with permission.

Emerging Consensus

At our first hearing, we observed a bipartisan consensus emerging around three themes:

First, there is agreement that parents must assume responsibility for their children. According to the U.S. Census Bureau, in 1983 there were 8.7 million women caring for children whose fathers were absent from the home. Only 58 percent of them had court orders or agreements to receive child support; 42 percent did not. Of the 58 percent with court orders, only half received the full amount due them, a quarter received partial payment, and the remaining quarter received nothing.

The problem affects mothers regardless of race, ethnicity, or region, although we do know that black mothers and mothers of Spanish origin living apart from the fathers of their children are less likely than their white counterparts to be awarded child support: 70 percent of white mothers are awarded child support payments, compared to 44 percent of Spanish-origin mothers, and 34 percent of black mothers. White mothers also receive larger child support payments per year ($2,475 in 1983), on average, than black ($1,465) and Spanish-origin ($1,839) mothers.

Child support enforcement is a responsibility that crosses income lines. All children are entitled to parental support. Yet, systematic enforcement of child support obligations is something we've just begun to do, despite the fact that Congress first passed child support legislation in 1950 (the Notification of Law Enforcement Officials, or the so-called NOLEO Amendment). But as these data show, we can and must do a better job of enforcing parental support obligations.

A second area of consensus has to do with work. Whether children live with both parents or just one, able-bodied parents have a responsibility to support their children by working. According to the Bureau of Labor Statistics, 70 percent of all mothers with children aged 6 to 18 years *are* working at jobs outside the home; more than half of all mothers with children under the age of six and even three are working. With so many mothers in the labor force, there is now general agreement that poor single mothers ought to work, at least part-time.

What is disturbing, however, is that many of these working mothers are still poor. In 1986, if a single parent with two children earned income equivalent to 75 percent of the poverty line, her earnings, together with AFDC and food stamp benefits, would have lifted her family above the poverty line in only eight states. Just ten years earlier, the same household would have escaped poverty in 46 states.

A single parent ought not to be poor and dependent on the welfare system when she is both working and fulfilling her child-rearing obligations. That is why I stress the importance of developing a new child support system that will rely, primarily, on parental support payments from the absent parent, plus earned income. Together, these sources of income ought to free mothers and their children from relying on public subsidies.

Should a combination of parental support payments and earnings still be insufficient to care adequately for these children, then time-limited government assistance, in the form of a child support supplement, ought to be made available. If, after a reasonable period of time (perhaps two years), a single mother has not secured a job, she would be provided a public work, training, or education assignment as a condition of continued public support.

A third source of agreement stems from the second: If we expect single parents to go to work, then we must put in place the supportive services that will enable them to train for, secure, and retain jobs outside of the home. For example, job-training and work experience programs, together with child care services are essential. There is also the matter of providing poor working parents with access to health care coverage for their families. We may have to mandate the extension of Medicaid benefits to poor households with young children, rather than leave that option to the states.

We Don't Have Children to Waste

In short, we are hearing a recurring theme, that of a new "social contract." A contract in which parents assume the primary financial responsibility for their children—absent parents by paying child support and custodial parents by working as much as is practicable. In exchange, the community, through temporary government assistance, will assure that children and the families raising them receive adequate income and health care.

A child should never be neglected, even in a society brimming with children. How much more careful we ought to be, then, as children become a scarce resource. Fifteen years ago, the birth rate in America fell below the level necessary to maintain the population. Quite simply, we cannot afford to waste a single child. And yet, at present, we suffer the impoverishment of 20 percent of our children. Do we expect children growing up in misery to mature into adults capable of maintaining, much less improving, American society? It ought not be left to chance.

RECOGNIZING AUTHOR'S POINT OF VIEW

This activity may be used as an individualized study guide for students in libraries and resource centers or as a discussion catalyst in small group and classroom discussions.

The capacity to recognize an author's point of view is an essential reading skill. Many readers do not make clear distinctions between descriptive articles that relate factual information and articles that express a point of view. Think about the readings in Chapter Three. Are these readings essentially descriptive articles that relate factual information or articles that attempt to persuade through editorial commentary and analysis?

Guidelines

1. Read through the following source descriptions. Choose one of the source descriptions that best describes each reading in Chapter Three.

Source Descriptions

a. **Essentially an article that relates factual information**
b. **Essentially an article that expresses editorial points of view**
c. **Both of the above**
d. **None of the above**

2. After careful consideration, pick out one source that you agree with the most. Be prepared to explain the reasons for your choice in a general class discussion.

3. Choose one of the source descriptions above that best describes the other readings in this book.

APPENDIX I

Work Program Activities

This material was excerpted from the United States General Accounting Office (GAO) report Work and Welfare: Current AFDC Work Programs and Implication for Federal Policy. *Members of the Human Resources Division of the GAO examined several areas of employment-related programs for welfare recipients, including work program activities. The GAO prepared the report for the Chairman of the House of Representatives Subcommittee on Intergovernmental Relations and Human Resources. The chairman requested information on employment-related programs for applicants and recipients of Aid to Families with Dependent Children (AFDC) benefits.*

* * *

Activities associated with work programs cluster in three groups based on assumptions their use implies about an individual's needs. Such activities encompass services for (1) job-ready participants, (2) needs other than skills, and (3) providing skills and education.

Services for Job-Ready Participants

Services for people needing little help to ready them for the job market include group and individual "job search" and "direct placement." Participants in individual job search look for employment largely on their own; in some programs, they report to program staff the number of employers contacted.

Group job search often includes a workshop in such job search techniques as resume preparation, interview skills, skill and interest assessment, and identifying potential employers. The workshop may be followed by use of a telephone bank, where participants call employers they have identified to seek employment. For some participants, job search workshops may serve a function more important than teaching a client how to look for a job—increasing the confidence of self-doubting individuals through peer support. We observed the final day of a San Diego workshop where participants critiqued videotapes of practice job interviews. Mutual support was evident throughout, but particularly in the participants' praise of one woman's progress in her interview. Though hesitant, her performance showed increased confidence from the first day when, the group said, she could barely explain that she was at the interview because she wanted a job.

In direct placement assistance, the program or another agency, usually the state Employment Service, seeks to place the client directly in a job. While group job search provides interaction with other participants and program staff and direct placement involves working with a program staff person, individual job search may be relatively unstructured and unsupervised. The three techniques are not mutually exclusive, but may be used in conjunction with each other.

Services for Needs Other Than Skills

Another service, work experience, introduces the person to work and some practical experience, generally without providing new skills. Programs can choose between the approaches offered by Community Work Experience Program (CWEP) and Work Incentive Program (WIN), as well as a hybrid of the two. Under the CWEP option, AFDC recipients work a number of hours that is usually determined by dividing their grants by the minimum wage. They may be assigned to this activity for unlimited amounts of time. While this can be viewed as a chance to require work in exchange for welfare (workfare in its narrow sense), some programs using the CWEP version of work experience also see it as a way to prepare people for employment. Under the WIN Program, work experience is seen as a full-time, short-term chance to brush up on skills and work habits. Participants in WIN work experience work full time, but are limited to 13-week assignments. A program may actually practice a hybrid of the two approaches to supplement WIN funding with uncapped CWEP funding. Thus, the hours worked might be determined as in a CWEP, but the assignment limited to a specific time period.

Programs may also see work experience as a form of on-the-job training or internship in which participants can develop skills while working for a supervisor. Work experience may be combined with classroom training, e.g., a New York City project alternated weeks of training in office skills with work experience in city agencies.

Most CWEP programs have been run on a small scale. However, there are some large CWEP projects, including one in New York City where about 3,000 AFDC recipients, joined with about 12,000 General Assistance recipients in a similar program, participate at any one time. This program illustrates the massive logistics of operating such a large scale program, which to some extent necessitates an impersonal nature. The program calls in about 18,000 people a month, placing them in assignments through a highly organized and regimented process. People assemble in a large room in a downtown welfare office; they may present program staff with reasons they cannot work. Representatives of agencies offering CWEP positions occupy rows of booths and interview AFDC recipients, accepting them or rejecting them immediately.

The use of work experience can be controversial, raising several questions. Some critics charge that CWEP workers displace regular workers, especially since work experience positions must be in public or private nonprofit agencies where tight budgets make "free" workers attractive. The CWEP approach is used most often in rural areas within states,[1] rather than in urban areas where opposition from unions, welfare advocacy groups, and municipal officials may be strong. For example, Pittsburgh and Philadelphia declined to participate in Pennsylvania's CWEP for these reasons. Some large cities, notably San Diego and New York City, do have CWEPs, however.

Critics also claim work experience is unfair to the people who perform work of value, but are not compensated as other workers are. Manpower Demonstration Research Corporation's (MDRC) studies of several programs that include work experience conclude the jobs were not "make work," but involved needed services.[2] Some positions actually may be the same as those of regular employees who receive pay higher than the minimum wage, the rate by which CWEP hours usually are calculated. Some programs, however, use the average or prevailing wage for a position rather than the minimum wage to calculate work hours.

Services Providing Skills and Education

The third group of services assumes participants need a skill, a credential such as a high school diploma or GED, or basic education. Participants may enter education and training services because the program's assessment identifies a need or in some cases because the client has chosen them. These services are offered in a variety of ways. Training may be in a classroom or on-the-job. The program itself may pay for the training or enrollees may be referred to training under the Job Training Partnership Act or the vocational education system.

On-the-job training (OJT) is sometimes subsidized by the recipient's welfare grant. This mechanism, called grant diversion, is now permitted under the work supplementation authority. Our survey identified 14 states that have begun operating work supplementation/grant diversion projects in the past few years. An MDRC study of grant diversion projects in six states found that these programs encounter problems reaching large numbers of people. Although grant diversion was appealing as a funding mechanism for OJT, the programs still had problems developing jobs in the private sector, especially in finding positions for individuals with serious barriers to employment.[3]

Another form of OJT often subsidized by the participant's grant is "supported work," which combines work experience with extensive counseling and group support. A multistate supported work experiment begun in the 1970s was found to benefit female long-term AFDC recipients with school-age children. (Those with children under age six were not included in the demonstration.)[4] These programs are expensive to operate, however, and largely are being phased out. Our review found supported work being offered in Massachusetts, West Virginia, California, Connecticut, and New York.

Education can mean anything from one-on-one tutoring in basic reading skills to a college education. A common strategy in programs we visited was to encourage participants to complete a GED program. In Oklahoma, adult education classes leading to a GED were held at the welfare office for participants' convenience. Some programs, however, were finding people with reading levels far below what the classes required. A few were experimenting with individual tutoring to try and raise skills quickly. In one South Carolina community, local college students acted as tutors. New York City contracted with a professor at Columbia University's Teachers College to upgrade reading and math skills in six weeks.

Staff of eight programs we visited said they would accept attendance at a community college or four-year college as participation. The programs did not necessarily pay for the education, but would help participants apply for state or federal aid, such as Pell Grants, while also supplying support services. We also found programs, however, that did not count college attendance as participation, believing that AFDC benefits should not subsidize lengthy degree programs.

[1] Demetra Smith Nightingale, *Federal Employment and Training Policy Changes During the Reagan Administration: State and Local Responses* (Washington, D.C.: The Urban Institute, 1985), p. 69.

[2] Judith M. Gueron, *Work Initiatives For Welfare Recipients: Lessons From a Multi-State Experiment* (New York: Manpower Demonstration Research Corporation, 1986), p. 25.

[3] Michael Bangser, James Healy, and Robert Ivry, *Welfare Grant Diversion: Lessons and Prospects* (New York: Manpower Demonstration Research Corporation, 1986), pp. 53-54.

[4] Stanley H. Masters and Rebecca Maynard, *The Impact of Supported Work On Long-Term Recipients of AFDC Benefits* (New York: Manpower Demonstration Research Corporation, 1981), pp. 25, 126.

APPENDIX II

New Welfare Reform Bill

On Tuesday, September 27, 1988, a House-Senate conference committee voted 35-8 to approve a compromise plan to overhaul the American welfare system.

The $3.34 billion welfare reform bill is designed to move welfare recipients into the work force through education, job training, and mandatory work programs. The bill has been referred to as a landmark piece of legislation because the work program would be the first of its kind in the welfare system's 53-year history.

Specifically, the bill provides for a strong job search component. The Job Opportunities and Basic Skills (JOBS) program is the centerpiece of the legislation. The program would require welfare parents with children over three years of age to enroll in state basic education, job search, and community service programs. This program would receive $600 million in federal funds in its first year.

The bill also offers recipients one year of day-care assistance and one year of continued family Medicaid after they have found a job and have worked their way off welfare.

In addition to these provisions, the bill seeks to improve the welfare parent's income by enforcing the payment of child support; this would be accomplished by requiring employers to automatically deduct court-ordered child support from the non-custodial parent's paycheck. Moreover, beginning in 1991, the bill would require that all states provide assistance to poor children living with both parents.

BIBLIOGRAPHY

Anderson, Martin. "Social Welfare Policy, The Objectives of the Reagan Administration," *The Social Contract Revisited: Aims and Outcomes of President Reagan's Social Welfare Policy,* D. Lee Bawden, ed. Washington, D.C.: The Urban Institute Press, 1984, pp. 1-16.

Auletta, Ken. *The Underclass.* New York: Vintage Books, 1983.

Bane, Mary Jo, and David T. Ellwood. *The Dynamics of Dependence: The Routes to Self-Sufficiency.* Washington, D.C.: U.S. Department of Health and Human Services, June 1983.

Bangser, Michael, James Healy, and Robert Ivry. *Welfare Grant Diversion, Early Observations From Programs In Six States.* New York: Manpower Demonstration Research Corporation, March 1985.

—————. *Welfare Grant Diversion, Lessons and Prospects.* New York: Manpower Demonstration Research Corporation, March 1986.

Bawden, D. Lee, Eugene P. Erickson, and Diana Davis. *A New Survey to Study Duration on AFDC.* Washington, D.C.: The Urban Institute, June 1984.

Berkeley Planning Associates. Administrative Release of Chapter 2 to *Evaluation Design Assessment of Work-Welfare Projects, Phase I: Final Report.* Washington, D.C.: U.S. Department of Health and Human Services, July 1981.

Blank, Helen. *Child Care: The States' Response. A Survey of State Child Care Policies, 1983-1984.* Washington, D.C.: Children's Defense Fund, 1984.

Blank, Helen, and Amy Wilkins. *Child Care: Whose Priority? A State Child Care Fact Book, 1985.* Washington, D.C.: Children's Defense Fund, 1985.

Burke, Vee. *Aid to Families With Dependent Children: Structural Change.* Washington, D.C.: U.S. Congressional Research Service, February 19, 1986.

—————. *Welfare Reform.* Washington, D.C.: U.S. Congressional Research Service, February 18, 1986.

Burtless, Gary. "Are Targeted Wage Subsidies Harmful? Evidence from a Wage Voucher Experiment," *Industrial and Labor Relations Review,* Vol. 39, No. 1 (October 1985), pp. 105-114.

——————. "Manpower Policies for the Disadvantaged: What Works?" *The Brookings Review,* Vol. 3, No. 1 (Fall 1984), pp. 18-22.

Children's Defense Fund. *A Children's Defense Fund Budget: An Analysis of the FY 1987 Federal Budget and Children.* Washington, D.C.: Children's Defense Fund, 1986.

——————. *Black and White Children in America.* Washington, D.C.: Children's Defense Fund, 1985.

Danziger, Sheldon, and Peter Gottschalk. "How Have Families with Children Been Faring?" Prepared for the Joint Economic Committee of the Congress. November 1985.

——————. "Work, Poverty, and the Working Poor." Prepared for the Employment and Housing Subcommittee of the House Committee on Government Operations. December 12, 1985.

Danziger, Sheldon, and Daniel H. Weinburg, ed. *Fighting Poverty: What Works and What Doesn't.* Cambridge, MA: Harvard University Press, 1986.

Duncan, Greg, and Saul D. Hoffman. "Welfare Dynamics and Welfare Policy: Past Evidence and Future Research Directions." Paper presented at the Association for Public Policy Analysis and Management meetings, Washington, D.C., October 1985.

Duncan, Greg J. *Years of Poverty, Years of Plenty: The Changing Economic Fortunes of American Workers and Families.* Ann Arbor, MI: Institute for Social Research, 1984.

Ellwood, David T. *Targeting "Would-Be" Long-Term Recipients of AFDC.* Washington, D.C.: U.S. Department of Health and Human Services, January 1986.

Ellwood, David T., and Mary Jo Bane. *The Impact Of AFDC On Family Structure and Living Arrangements.* Washington, D.C.: U.S. Department of Health and Human Services, March 1984.

Fremont-Smith, Lee Bowes. "Employment Demonstrations: A Strategy for Policy Formulation," *Applied Poverty Research,* Goldstein, Richard and Stephen M. Sachs, eds. Totowa, NJ: Rowman and Allanheld, Publishers, 1983, pp. 260-268.

Friedman, Barry, et al. *An Evaluation Of The Massachusetts Work Experience Program.* Waltham, MA: Center for Employment and Income Studies, Brandeis University, October 1980.

Friedman, Dana. "Corporate Financial Assistance for Child Care," *The Conference Board Research Bulletin,* No. 177. 1985.

Garvin, Charles D., Audrey D. Smith, and William J. Reid. *The Work Incentive Experience.* New York: Universe Books, 1978.

Ginzberg, Eli, ed. *Employing the Unemployed.* New York: Basic Books, 1980.

Goldman, Barbara, Daniel Friedlander, and David Long. *Final Report On The San Diego Job Search And Work Experience Demonstration.* New York: Manpower Demonstration Research Corporation, February 1986.

Goldman, Barbara, et al. *Findings From The San Diego Job Search And Work Experience Demonstration.* New York: Manpower Demonstration Research Corporation, March 1985.

————. *Preliminary Findings From The San Diego Job Search And Work Experience Demonstration.* New York: Manpower Demonstration Research Corporation, February 1984.

Goodwin, Leonard. *Causes and Cures of Welfare, New Evidence on the Social Psychology of the Poor.* Lexington, MA: Lexington Books, 1983.

Grossman, Jean Baldwin, and Audrey Mirsky. *A Survey of Recent Programs Designed to Reduce Long-Term Welfare Dependency.* Washington, D.C.: U.S. Department of Health and Human Services, 1985.

Grossman, Jean Baldwin, Rebecca Maynard, and Judith Roberts. *Reanalysis Of The Effects Of Selected Employment and Training Programs For Welfare Recipients.* Washington, D.C.: U.S. Department of Health and Human Services, October 1985.

Gueron, Judith M. *Work Initiatives for Welfare Recipients: Lessons From A Multi-State Experiment.* New York: Manpower Demonstration Research Corporation, February 24, 1986.

Gueron, Judith M., and Richard P. Nathan. "The MDRC Work/Welfare Project: Objectives, Status, Significance," *Policy Studies Review,* Vol. 4, No. 3 (February 1985), pp. 417-432.

Harrington, Michael. *The New American Poverty.* New York: Holt, Rinehart and Winston, 1984.

Hoffreth, Sandra L., and Freya L. Sonenstein. *An Examination of the Effects of Alternative Approaches to Financing Day Care for AFDC Children, Final Report.* Washington, D.C.: U.S. Department of Health and Human Services, August 10, 1983.

Hollister, Robinson G., Jr., Peter Kemper, and Rebecca A. Maynard, eds. *The National Supported Work Demonstration.* Madison, WI: The University of Wisconsin Press, 1984.

Kamerman, Sheila B. "Child-care Services: A National Picture," *Monthly Labor Review,* Vol. 108, No. 12 (December 1983), pp. 35-39.

Koshel, Jeffrey. *Work Programs for Welfare Recipients—Issues and Options.* Washington, D.C.: Center for Policy Research, National Governors' Association, April 1984.

Levitan, Sar A. *Programs in Aid of the Poor for the 1980s.* Baltimore, MD: Johns Hopkins University Press, 1980.

Leyser, Barbara, Adele M. Blong, and Judith Riggs. *Beyond The Myths, The Families Helped By The AFDC Program.* Second Edition. Washington, D.C.: Center on Social Welfare Policy and Law, 1985.

Linden, Barbara, and Deborah C. Vincent. *Workfare in Theory and Practice.* Washington, D.C.: National Social Science and Law Center, Inc., 1982.

Mason, Jan, John S. Wodarski, and T. M. Jim Parham. "Work and Welfare: A Reevaluation of AFDC," *Social Work,* Vol. 30, No. 3 (May-June, 1985), pp. 197-203.

Masters, Stanley H., and Rebecca Maynard. *The Impact of Supported Work On Long-Term Recipients Of AFDC Benefits.* New York: Manpower Demonstration Research Corporation, February 1981.

Maynard, Rebecca, and Myles Maxfield, Jr. *A Design Of A Social Demonstration Of Targeted Employment Services For AFDC Recipients.* Washington, D.C.: U.S. Department of Health and Human Services, June 13, 1986.

Maxfield, Myles, Jr., and Mark Rucci. *A Simulation Model Of Targeted Employment And Training Programs For Long Term Welfare Recipients: Technical Documentation.* Washington, D.C.: U.S. Department of Health and Human Services, January 6, 1986.

Mead, Lawrence M. *Beyond Entitlement, The Social Obligations of Citizenship.* New York: The Free Press, 1986.

Meiklejohn, Nanine. "Work and Training Opportunities for Welfare Recipients." Statement before the Subcommittee on Public Assistance and Unemployment Compensation of the House Ways and Means Committee, June 17, 1986.

Mitchell, John J., Mark Lincoln Chadwin and Demetra Smith Nightingale. *Implementing Welfare-Employment Programs: An Institutional Analysis of The Work Incentive (WIN) Program.* Washington, D.C.: Urban Institute, October 1979.

Moynihan, Daniel Patrick. *Family and Nation.* New York: Harcourt Brace Jovanovich, 1986.

Murray, Charles. *Losing Ground, American Social Policy, 1950-1980.* New York: Basic Books, 1984.

Nelson, Hal. *Evaluation of the Community Work Experience Program.* Olympia, WA: Department of Social and Health Services, 1984.

Nightingale, Demetra Smith. *Federal Employment and Training Policy Changes During the Reagan Administration: State and Local Responses.* Washington, D.C.: The Urban Institute, May 1985.

O'Neill, June A., Douglas A. Wolf, Laurie J. Bassi, and Michael T. Hannan. *An Analysis of Time on Welfare.* Washington, D.C.: U.S. Department of Health and Human Services, June 1984.

Patterson, James T. *America's Struggle Against Poverty: 1900-1980.* Cambridge, MA: Harvard University Press, 1981.

Pearce, Diana M. "The Feminization of Ghetto Poverty," *Society,* Vol. 21, No. 1 (Nov./Dec. 1983), pp. 70-79.

Pennsylvania Department of Public Welfare, *Evaluation of Pennsylvania Community Work Experience Program.* Philadelphia: The Department, January 1986.

Piven, Frances Fox, and Richard A. Cloward. *Regulating the Poor, the Functions of Public Welfare.* New York: Vintage Books, 1971.

Rank, Mark R. "Exiting from Welfare: A Life-Table Analysis," *Social Science Review,* Vol. 59, No. 3 (September 1985), pp. 358-376.

Rein, Mildred. *Dilemmas of Welfare Policy, Why Work Strategies Haven't Worked.* New York: Praeger Publishers, 1982.

Schiller, Bradley R. *The Economics of Poverty and Discrimination.* Englewood Cliffs, NJ: Prentice-Hall, 1980.

Solow, Katherine, and Gary Walker. *The Job Training Partnership Act, Service to Women.* New York: Grinker, Walker and Associates, 1986.

U.S. House. Committee on Government Operations. *Opportunities for Self-Sufficiency For Women In Poverty.* 99th Cong., 1st sess. H. Rept. 99-459. Washington, D.C.: GPO, 1985.

U.S. House. Committee on Ways and Means. *Background Material and Data on Programs Within the Jurisdiction of the Committee on Ways and Means.* 99th Cong. 2nd sess. Washington, D.C.: GPO, 1986.

—————. *Children in Poverty.* 99th Cong., 1st sess. Washington, D.C.: GPO, 1985.

U.S. House. Subcommittee on Oversight and Subcommittee on Public Assistance and Unemployment Compensation. Committee on Ways and Means. *Families in Poverty: Changes in the "Safety Net."* 98th Cong., 2nd sess. Washington, D.C.: GPO, 1984.

U.S. House Subcommittee on Intergovernmental Relations and Human Resources, Committee on Government Operations. *Barriers to Self-Sufficiency for Single Female Heads of Families.* Hearings. 99th Cong., 1st sess. Washington, D.C.: GPO, 1985.

U.S. Congressional Budget Office. *Reducing Poverty Among Children.* Washington, D.C.: The Office, May 1985.

U.S. Congressional Budget Office and National Commission for Employment Policy. *CETA Training Programs: Do They Work For Adults?* Washington, D.C.: The Office, July 1982.

U.S. General Accounting Office. *An Evaluation of the 1981 AFDC Changes. Final Report.* PEMD-85-4. July 2, 1985.

——————. *An Overview of the WIN Program: Its Objectives, Accomplishments, And Problems.* HRD-22-85. June 21, 1982.

——————. *CWEP's Implementation Results To Date Raise Questions About The Administration's Proposed Mandatory Workfare Program.* PEMD-84-2. April 2, 1984.

——————. *Does AFDC Workfare Work? Information Is Not Yet Available From HHS's Demonstration Projects.* IPE-83-3. January 24, 1983.

——————. *Evidence Is Insufficient To Support The Administration's Proposed Changes To AFDC Programs.* HRD-85-92. August 27, 1985.

——————. *States Use Several Strategies To Cope With Funding Reductions Under Social Services Block Grant.* HRD-84-68, August 9, 1984.

Walker, Gary, Hilary Feldstein, and Katherine Solow. *An Independent Sector Assessment Of The Job Training Partnership Act.* New York: Grinker, Walker and Associates, January 1985.

Weitzman, Lenore J. *The Divorce Revolution: The Unexpected Social and Economic Consequences for Women and Children in America.* New York: The Free Press, 1985.

"Welfare and Work," *Public Welfare,* Vol. 44, No. 1. (Winter 1986).

White, Richard N. *Assessment of a WIN Quality Training Demonstration Project.* Washington, D.C.: Bureau of Social Science Research, Inc., April 1980.

Wicks, Anne B., and Carla M. Caro. *Factors Affecting the Employability of Welfare Recipients, A Survey of Women Receiving Aid to Families with Dependent Children Benefits in Washington State.* Washington, D.C.: National Social Science and Law Center, Inc., 1986.